GHOSTS OF THE WEST
TALES AND LEGENDS FROM THE BONANZA TRAIL

GHOSTS OF THE WEST
TALES AND LEGENDS FROM THE BONANZA TRAIL
✦

E. S. KNIGHTCHILDE

KNIGHT SKY PICTURES™
ESTES PARK, COLORADO

Ghosts of the West: Tales and Legends from the Bonanza Trail

Copyright © 2023, 2019 by E. S. Knightchilde

All rights reserved. No part of this book may be reproduced, utilized, or transmitted in any form or by any means, electronic or mechanical, including photocopying, or recording, or by any information storage and retrieval system, without permission in writing from the author or Knight Sky Pictures®. For more information, visit www.KnightSkyPictures.com.

Portions of this book were based on the screenplays of the *Ghosts of the West* documentary film series. The filmmakers relied upon accounts of certain events and persons from various sources purporting to be knowledgeable. Gross exaggeration was commonplace in contemporary accounts of nearly every aspect of life on the western frontier, often heavily obscuring accuracy and adding elements of fiction to historical truth. The filmmakers strove to reconcile numerous conflicting stories of the characteristics ascribed to the incidents and persons portrayed in the films, in many cases confronted with no reliable way of separating truth from folklore. Consequently, some aspects of the people, events, and interactions depicted (and their names) may be colored by faded memories, exaggeration, and incomplete accounts resulting in occasional unintentional fiction.

SECOND EDITION

Library of Congress Control Number: 2023933252

To Todd,
for his unending patience and unwavering support

"The Old West is not a certain place in a certain time, it's a state of mind. It's whatever you want it to be."

—Tom Mix

CONTENTS

PREFACE XI

ACKNOWLEDGMENTS XV

INTRODUCTION 1

ACT ONE: DISCOVERY 3
   AN AMERICAN RIVER IN MEXICO 3
   PROSPECTING PACK ANIMALS 7
   FALLING INTO SILVER 8
   A LUCKY SHOT AT RICHES 8

ACT TWO: BOOM 11
   GOLD FOR THE TAKING 12
   PATRIOTISM BY ANY OTHER NAME 15
   CALIFORNIA SECESSIONISTS 17

HENRY PLUMMER AND THE VIGILANCE COMMITTEE 18
HELL WITH THE FIRES OUT 20
THE PIRACY OF THE DENVER & RIO GRANDE RAILROAD 21
A CITY IN TWO STATES 22
A SEA OF SIN 24
A LADY CALLED SILVER HEELS 29

ACT THREE: BUST 37

THE PANIC OF '93 38
A TALE OF TWO CARSONS 41
THE FATE OF SILVER CLIFF 42
THE HOMESTAKE 44
SUNSET FOR THE CITY OF THE DAWN 45

ACT FOUR: GHOST 51

A SEA OF FIRE 51
NIGHTFALL FOR THE CITY OF THE DAWN 67

ACT FIVE: LOST 75

THE LOST BLUE BUCKET PLACERS 75
THE CRYPTOGRAM AND THE HIDDEN CACHE 76
TREASURE AND TRAGEDY ON SLATE MOUNTAIN 77
THE LOST DUTCHMAN MINE 78

AFTERWORD 81

APPENDICES 83

I: SUMMITVILLE, BODIE, AND THE HOMESTAKE MINE 85
II: BODIE, CALIFORNIA: JULY 4, 1880 89
III: "GOOD-BY, GOD..." 95
IV: REMINISCENCES OF BUCKSKIN JOE 97

BIBLIOGRAPHY 99

PHOTO CREDITS 103

MORE ON THE GHOST TOWNS OF THE OLD WEST 105

ABOUT THE AUTHOR 110

PREFACE

Even today, the Westward Road calls us...

When I was a 9-year-old living on the east coast, a juvenile mystery novel gathering dust on a classroom bookshelf captured my attention. I long since have forgotten its title and details, but the setting of an old west ghost town and a lost mine hidden in the hills beyond has remained undimmed in my imagination. Perhaps two years after that (and utterly unrelated), I "convinced" my parents that a used 8mm movie camera might be the only suitable gift for my upcoming birthday. I was soon shooting every vacation and family event for which I could afford to buy film.

Decades later, I was living in Colorado. While out of town for a wedding, a conversation with friends turned to the subject of ghost towns and an abandoned silver camp nearby. It is my only memory of that evening, and I will never forget my visit the following day—of how I stood in front of a weathered old building with its open doors and vacant windows and felt that it somehow stared back at me.

I embarked on a few road trip vacations, visiting every ghost town I could find and capturing many of them on black-and-white motion picture film. Though cutting together a unique vacation home movie was my original goal, the passing years saw the road trips grow in scope; and the amount of footage I accumulated became less the material for a three-minute film and more a testament to my chronic illness as a "ghost town junkie."

That initial feeling that the buildings somehow stared back still haunted me, and I eventually felt compelled to speak for that which has no voice. More than a decade after that first visit, test screenings were held for the feature documentary *Ghosts of the West: The End of the Bonanza Trail*.

The movie first received positive reviews from audiences, then critical acclaim, and theatres showing it began to sell out. Despite the original outline of the material calling for two (possibly three) installments, the completed film was deliberately written to stand on its own without a prequel or sequel. After a highly successful theatrical roadshow, I decided to move forward with production on the next film.

Above: Hundreds of moviegoers wait in line for the official cast and crew premiere of Ghosts of the West: The End of the Bonanza Trail in Denver, Colorado, 2013.

Opposite page: Theatrical release poster.

In May 2017, an article about the ongoing documentary project published in *Colorado Life Magazine* gained the notice of the Niwot Historical Society, which then invited me to present a program on ghost towns to their community. At the lecture's conclusion and with nearly the exact words as had been written on one of the test audience comment cards several years earlier, an attendee remarked: "You should write a book." Regarding myself as a filmmaker rather than an author, I did not give it much consideration until an invitation arrived from the historic Colorado Chautauqua in Boulder, and their programmer casually asked if I happened to have a book. After scheduling had been arranged and deliverables delivered, the thought of printed matter bound by more than a set of brass-plated fasteners returned. Between the stack of notecards on my desk and script material either discarded or in use, I realized that a substantial amount of the potential volume sat before me.

What follows is based in part upon the text of the lecture *Ghost Towns of the American West*, the script for Best Documentary Award-winner *Ghosts of the West: The End of the Bonanza Trail*, and the research for and production of the forthcoming film *Ghosts of the West: Stampede on the Bonanza Trail*. This book is not intended to be a travel guide or an exhaustive history; rather, it is "edutainment" with some data and images to enhance the telling of anecdotes, stories, and legends. If you are planning a trip of your own, you can find many excellent regional books containing well-organized itineraries at your local bookseller.

For truly in-depth histories, I recommend works dedicated to a single town or event. Ideal examples of the former are *Aurora, Nevada: 1860-*

1960 (Second Edition) by Clifford Alpheus Shaw and *Aurora, Nevada's Silent City on the Hill* by Sue Silver. A related example of a work about a single event is *The Last Days of the Daly Gang at Aurora, Nevada*, also by Clifford Alpheus Shaw. Together these books provide a comprehensive picture of the city's history, life during its boom-and-bust years, and those who lived and died in the town and still rest in its cemetery.

An example of a work focused on a specific moment is *Calamity: The Heppner Flood of 1903* by Joann Green Byrd. Though the town is not represented in these pages, Byrd's account is captivating and recommended reading.

◆

The main body of the volume in your hands is organized into five sections. The first relates some brief tales of discovery; the middle three contain stories of towns and camps as they passed through boom times, hard times, and on to their final fates. (Some sites appear across multiple sections to illustrate progress through the discovery-boom-bust-ghost cycle.) The final chapter bookends the first with tales of lost discoveries and caches, for which some still search.

Lastly, while this book, the lecture, and the films all necessarily overlap to some degree, none are wholly duplicated, and interested parties can find new and supplementary information in each. There are many stories related to ghost towns, for instance, that, due to their modernity, fall outside the scope of the entire project. This volume's appendices include one such account that reveals a surprising connection between two sites separated by over one thousand road miles.

I hope you find the selected tales and additional photographs of this second edition enjoyable.

–E. S. Knightchilde
Still somewhere on a western road,
March 20, 2023

ACKNOWLEDGMENTS

Only through the generous support of archivists, authors, librarians, and others located throughout the western states was this book made possible, along with the films and lecture series on which it is partially based. While the complete list of those individuals and organizations is quite long, the following provided invaluable assistance during the research, filming, or photographing of sites covered in this volume:

Karalea Clough, Nevada Historical Society
Eric Dillingham, District Archeologist, Bridgeport Ranger District, U.S. Forest Service
Coi E. Drummond-Gehrig, Denver Public Library Western History Collection
Robert Frenchu
The Ghost Town Club of Colorado
Joshua D. Heitzmann, Supervising Ranger, Bodie State Historic Park
Cindy Huelsman, South Park Historical Foundation
Blake MacKenzie
Lory Morrow, Montana Historical Society
Arlene Melton, Central Nevada Historical Society
Park County Local History Archives
Todd Prescott
Clifford Alpheus Shaw, author, *Aurora, Nevada: 1860-1960*
Sue Silver, author, *Aurora Nevada's Silent City on the Hill*
Elena Smith, California State Library, Sacramento
Kent Stoddard, Mono County Historical Society
TJ Vietor, Granite County Museum
Christie Wright, author, *All That Lies Beneath*
Kellyn Younggren, Montana Historical Society

The following individuals and several anonymous donors contributed to the Kickstarter fundraising campaign in February and March 2019 to cover the usage fees associated with the historical images herein. Without their generous support and belief, the first edition of this book may never have been published.

Lee Dahl and Joan Fields – Leisure West Tours

Anthony D'Amico	E. S. Segil
Andrew D'Amico	Andrew and Frances D'Amico
Cathy Moore	Wayne and Denise Dreyer
Philip G. Horey	Sally Alt
Scott and René Booker	Timothy Condon
Christopher Davis	Melissa Renae
Adrian L. Hernandez	Rebekah Kass
Jeff Olbertz	Ryan and Angie Prescott
Christie Wright	Brian Connors
Kathy Monroe Koehler	Darrell Arndt
Norman L. Brown	Jonathan G. Grice
Patrick O'Hara	Leslie Simpson
Dean Williams	Timothy Brazzell
Ken Nagasako	Seán Doherty
Travis Heath	Keith Kirby
Alexander Lucard	Beth Mañalac
Ray Martorella	Amy McKnight and Eric Matelski
John Mulder	John Mulhouse, City of Dust
Kylie N.	Jeremy Poley
Christian Rider	Janice Stice
Robert Suizu	Susie Taylor
Jenny Wilde	Matt Yaeger

Finally, I owe great thanks to historian Christie Wright, who offered invaluable feedback during the research and writing of the sections on Buckskin Joe, Colorado.

GHOSTS OF THE WEST
TALES AND LEGENDS FROM THE BONANZA TRAIL

INTRODUCTION

You will find it hard to believe that there stood at one time a fiercely-flourishing little city, of two thousand or three thousand souls, with its newspaper, fire company, brass band, volunteer militia, bank, hotels, noisy Fourth of July processions and speeches, gambling hells crammed with tobacco smoke, profanity, and rough-bearded men of all nations and colors, with tables heaped with gold dust sufficient for the revenues of a German principality—streets crowded and rife with business—town lots worth four hundred dollars a front foot—labor, laughter, music, dancing, swearing, fighting, shooting, stabbing—a bloody inquest and a man for breakfast every morning—everything that delights and adorns existence—all the appointments and appurtenances of a thriving and prosperous and promising young city,—and now nothing is left of it all but a lifeless, homeless solitude. The men are gone, the houses have vanished, even the name of the place is forgotten. In no other land, in modern times, have towns so absolutely died and disappeared...

—Mark Twain, *Roughing It*, 1872

♦

What is a ghost town? Merriam-Webster defines it as "a once-flourishing town wholly or nearly deserted usually as a result of the exhaustion of some natural resource." Under such strict classification, only sites like Bodie, California; Bannack, Montana; and Rhyolite, Nevada, would qualify.

In contrast, many ghost town enthusiasts and historians prefer to broaden the definition and include populated towns that are mere shadows of what they once were, as well as those that have utterly vanished. Sites such as Virginia City, Montana; Gold Hill, Nevada; and Bachelor, Colorado, would be included under those guidelines.

But a clinical approach does not address the fascination ghost towns hold, even for those who care little for history. Perhaps it is the way they play upon the imagination—the way the ghosts of the past feel so close that if you squint your eyes just right when the light is low, you can almost see the town and its inhabitants at the uttermost limit of vision.

Many nineteenth-century camps died within years and sometimes months of being born. Even as Mark Twain was writing *Roughing It*, the ghost towns were there for him to see. And with oft-told legends routinely accepted as fact, it can be somewhat problematic, if not impossible, to separate truth from fiction.

Accompanied by historical and contemporary photos, herein are some tales that may offer insight into the reasons behind our fascination. So sit back and relax—squint your mind's eye if you must—and let the Ghosts of the West step out from amongst the shadows and stand undimmed in your imagination.

The view at Gilmore, ID.

ACT ONE: DISCOVERY

The principal amusement here during the winter has been card playing, telling yarns, and drinking the most execrable whiskey.
—H. L. Bolton, January 19, 1859

Miners and prospectors loved a good yarn, and tales often grew in the telling. As one wry-witted Englishman noted, some individuals beyond the frontier line held "such excessive regard for the truth that they use[d] it with penurious frugality."

If some discovery stories are to be believed, prospectors, more often than not, stumbled over rich claims or were led to them by wayward pack animals. At times, the finders of great wealth were not looking for gold—and even folklore's cacophonous echo chamber could not drown out the facts.

An American River in Mexico

In 1834, Swiss immigrant Johann August Suter sailed from France to

North America, where he would call himself John Augustus Sutter for the rest of his life. Over the next five years, he traveled from New York City to St. Louis, Santa Fe (then part of Mexico), Oregon Territory, and even the Kingdom of Hawaii. His final stop brought him to the northern part of Mexico's pastoral backwater province, Alta California. There he began construction on a fortified settlement named New Helvetia at the future site of Sacramento.

Top: Diorama of Sutter's Fort, Sutter's Fort State Historic Park, Sacramento, California.
Bottom: Interior courtyard, Sutter's Fort State Historic Park, Sacramento, California.

Above: John Sutter's office, Sutter's Fort State Historic Park, Sacramento, California.
Below: Reconstruction of Sutter's Mill, Marshall Gold Discovery State Historic Park, Coloma, California.

About six years later, New Jersey-born James Wilson Marshall arrived on a wagon train from Oregon. Sutter and Marshall soon began working together. On May 16, 1847, Sutter directed Marshall to head to the foothills and select a site for a sawmill.

Marshall chose a spot on the South Fork of the American River and commenced work in September. Construction proceeded as planned, with Marshall checking the job each morning. Of the fateful day of January 24, 1848, he later wrote:

> *After shutting off the water from the race I stepped into it, near the lower end, and there, upon the rock, about six inches beneath the surface of the water, I discovered the gold. I was entirely alone at the time. I picked up one or two pieces and examined them attentively; and having some general knowledge of minerals, I could not call to mind more than two which in any way resembled this—sulphuret of iron, very bright and brittle; and gold, bright, yet malleable; I then tried it between two rocks, and found that it could be beaten into a different shape, but not broken. I then collected four or five pieces and went up to Mr. Scott (who was working at the carpenter's bench making the mill wheel) with the pieces in my hand and said, "I have found it."*

The discovery behind those four words sparked what has been called the greatest mass migration in history, the effects of which will be discussed in the next chapter. In the meantime, three more stories of discovery follow, which (unlike Marshall's account) probably contain a significant measure of tall tale. A grain of salt is recommended when evaluating the amount of truth in each.

A stone monument (base seen at right) marks the original location of John Sutter's sawmill on the South Fork of the American River in Coloma.

Prospecting Pack Animals

In March 1851, prospectors from Oregon Territory broke camp in northern California when something remarkable—but not unprecedented in the history of discoveries—happened. A mule pulled up a clump of grass while grazing alongside the trail. Abraham Thompson noticed telltale flecks amongst the roots, panned some dirt, and found gold. The site became known as Thompson's Dry Diggings and would grow into the modern town of Yreka.

Now consider that these prospectors had camped where gold could be found by scratching away some topsoil but had not made the discovery ahead of their mules. And while the accepted story casts some doubt on the group's skill set, merely stating that they had found gold while breaking camp is not (admittedly) as entertaining to tell around a fire or card game.

Miners at Thompson's Dry Diggings, California, circa 1851.

Falling into Silver

In her book *Stampede to Timberline*, Muriel Sibell Wolle relates that two men staked out the Johnny Bull mining claim in the Wet Mountain Valley of Colorado Territory in 1868. They dug a prospect hole to a depth of ten feet, then gave up and left.

Ten years later, a prospector was checking the area near the Johnny Bull, lost his footing, and fell forward. Driving a pick into the ground stopped his fall; upon retrieving it, he noticed bits of galena, an important ore of lead and silver. He then dug seven feet into solid galena ore.

Before continuing, take a moment to visualize that circumstance.

A Lucky Shot at Riches

According to folklore, the camp of Buckskin Joe, situated in the western portion of Kansas Territory that later became Colorado Territory, began with the accidental discovery of gold in the latter half of 1859. Joseph Higganbottam (aka Higganbotham and numerous other spelling variations, but called "Buckskin Joe" due to his choice of clothing) was out hunting when he sighted a deer or elk. Believing he had hit the animal after firing, the man searched for the blood trail. The stories do not say whether he ever caught up with his prey, but they *do* claim he found the bullet lodged in an outcrop of gold.

Some variations on the discovery story place the hunt during the winter, occasionally with a bear as the intended target. Higganbottam slipped in the snow; his shot went wild, and the bullet grazed the side of a hill, revealing a rich gold deposit. Unfortunately for that comedic account, it is unlikely that a bear had been roaming around in the winter, and an earlier source states that the discovery occurred in the summer. (Summer snows, however, are not unknown in the high country of the Rocky Mountains.)

At its heart, the tale strains credulity, yet similar stories are told of discoveries in several other Old West camps.

The ruins of an arrastra in a stream near the site of Buckskin Joe, Colorado.

The illegal camp of Deadwood in the Black Hills of Lakota Territory, 1876.

ACT TWO: BOOM

They made us many promises, more than I can remember, but they never kept but one; they promised to take our land, and they took it.
—Elderly Sioux to a white minister

News of a mineral strike spread as quickly as population and transportation would allow. Miners, merchants, ministers, thieves, and soiled doves would flock to the new diggings, regardless of whether doing so was legal. Such was the case in the Black Hills after Lieutenant Colonel George Armstrong Custer led the U.S. Army into Lakota Territory, as defined in the 1868 Treaty of Fort Laramie, and announced the existence of gold in 1874.

At left is the illegal mining camp of Deadwood in 1876. The United States unilaterally stripped the Hills from the Sioux Nation in 1877.

General William T. Sherman (facing, third from left) and commissioners in council with Indian chiefs at Ft. Laramie, Wyoming Territory, 1868.

GOLD FOR THE TAKING

I adhere to my long settled conviction that, next to outright and indisputable gambling, the hardest (though sometimes the quickest) way to obtain gold is to mine for it...

—Horace Greeley

Despite some initial attempts to keep it quiet, news of the January 24 strike at Sutter's Mill eventually spread around the world. On February 2, nine days after discovery, the Mexican-American War ended by treaty, with Mexico ceding more than half of its pre-1836 territory, including Alta California, to the U.S., as shown in the illustration below.

The above map of the U.S. and the territories acquired at the close of the Mexican-American War accompanied President Polk's annual message to Congress in 1848.

In 1848 with a total non-native population of approximately fourteen thousand, California saw about four hundred people immigrating into the Territory and about two thousand living on and working along the river banks. It has been said that gold at the time was so plentiful and seemingly inexhaustible that the area was nearly free of crime. Gold was left unguarded in tents, and a shovel or pick in a hole indicated ownership.

At least eighty-five thousand more fortune hunters arrived the following year, and ships in San Francisco's harbor were abandoned when entire crews deserted for the gold fields. Some vessels were used as hotels or for storage; others were sunk. As the village of about 800 rapidly expanded, the growing settlement built over many submerged ships.

By 1852, San Francisco had grown into a city of 34,776, and California's population had skyrocketed to nearly a quarter million. The gold-seekers came from the Americas, western and central Europe, China, and even the Kingdom of Hawaii.

Some immigrants had additional incentives to head to the Pacific coast of the New World. Around the same time as James Marshall was making his discovery in Mexico, the Great Famine had caused deaths estimated to number in the hundreds of thousands, and much of Europe was poised to explode into revolution. Beginning in Sicily on January 12 and continuing as the year progressed, the middle and lower classes from France to Hungary rebelled against foreign and domestic conservative rulers, demanding independence, greater freedom, and in some cases, a constitutional republic. Instability from revolutions and counter-revolutions lasting into 1849 and an ongoing famine would prompt people to seek a better life as much as, if not more than, "free" gold.

As would happen to the Sioux in the 1870s and was often the case during the nineteenth century, gold-seekers paid little heed to John Sutter's property or rights. They overran his land, slaughtered his livestock, destroyed his crops, and cut his timber. He would spend many of his remaining years seeking restitution for his losses, and James Marshall would die a pauper not far from the site of his discovery.

Abandoned ships in San Francisco harbor during the Gold Rush. Combined from two separate photographs.

There will be an immense crowd of gold seekers. They must naturally be skinned. Fellow citizens, let us prepare to do the skinning.
—*Los Angeles News,* during the 1870 San Diego County gold rush

Limited supply, increasing demand, high transportation costs from the States to the Territories, and a generous amount of available gold (not to mention greed) combined to create an inflationary effect on just about everything in the camps during the nineteenth-century rushes, as evidenced by the prices of some essential items like those below.

Standing atop a tall column on a hill above Coloma, a statue of James Marshall points to the site of the gold discovery. Marshall Gold Discovery State Historic Park, Coloma, California.

California Mining Camps, 1848

Butter & Cheese	up to $6/pound
Shirts	$16 each
Shirts laundered	$1 each
Blankets	$50 - $100 each
Horses	$100 - $150 each

Coloma, California Territory, 1848-50

Picks	up to $6/pound
Shovels	$16 each

San Francisco, California, 1850s

Eggs	$1 each
Whiskey	$40/quart
Sleep on a cot in a crowded room	$8/night

Rocker, Montana Territory, 1860s

Apples	$0.50 each
Grapes	$10/pound

Bannack, Montana Territory, 1860s

Nails	$1 each
8 x 10 panes of glass	$1 each
Sugar, coffee, bacon	$1/pound
Flour	$25/100-pound sack
Flour in winter	$100/100-pound sack

For perspective on the above, gold was usually traded or valued between $16 and $18 per ounce at the time. Back in the States, where extreme issues of supply and demand, transportation, and large amounts of gold were not present, the prices for similar goods were significantly lower.

<u>Eastern States</u>

Blankets	$2 each
Sugar	$0.09/pound
Bacon	$0.10/pound
Flour	$3 per 100-pound sack

PATRIOTISM BY ANY OTHER NAME

No matter where gold or silver rushes led in the ensuing decades, prospectors and miners far beyond the western frontier often yearned for home. The names they chose for their camps, such as Como and Richmond, were sometimes a nod to their origins. On occasion, they went a step further and stated where their sympathies lay during the War Between the States.

In July 1866, a group primarily composed of Southerners founded Leesburg, Idaho Territory—a camp named in honor of their Confederate hero, General Robert E. Lee. Those arriving later bristled at the name and called their settlement at the upper end of town "Grantsville" in support of the Union.

The community survived into the 1940s before it was finally abandoned. Today the Grantsville side (right portion of photo) holds two residences, one built after 1900 and the other likely moved from another area. On the other hand, the Leesburg side contains the cemetery and the remains of 18 structures, including the post office, schoolhouse, hotel, tax

Panoramic view of Leesburg and Grantsville, Idaho (left and right of the dashed line, respectively).

assessor's office, mercantile, butcher shop, boarding house, and stagecoach office. And while the Confederate cause was lost, the name given to the camp by the Southerners was not. It eventually won out for the entire site as the decades passed.

Leesburg butcher shop, post office, schoolhouse, and tax assessor's office.

Newspapers used as insulation to keep out cold drafts still adorn the walls of the post office. Though the ad at right dates from the twentieth century, it calls to mind another effect of the profound isolation many gold-seekers beyond the frontier line felt: Independence Day was celebrated intensely, sometimes with festivities that lasted for days.

Aside from parades, typical highlights included: readings from the Constitution and Declaration of Independence; orations; igniting gunpowder; foot races; horse races; drilling competitions; climbing greased poles; and attempting to capture oiled pigs. (For an account of a celebration at Bodie, California, see Appendix II, pp. 89-94.)

Yet, as illustrated in the following tale,

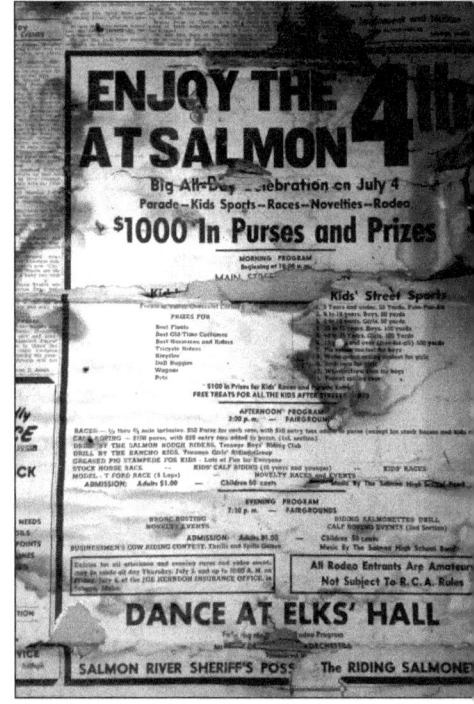

Newspaper insulation on post office walls.

all that patriotism did not dissuade the miners of one California Gold Rush camp from making a drastic decision one early spring day.

CALIFORNIA SECESSIONISTS

The town of Rough and Ready was founded in 1849 and named after the recently-elected President of the United States, General Zachary Taylor, who had borne the nickname "Old Rough and Ready" during the Mexican-American War. The legend begins with most townspeople being Southern sympathizers who objected to California's entry into the Union but more so to a government-imposed mining tax "on all claims." In a hotheaded moment, the residents voted to secede from the United States on April 7, 1850, and establish The Great Republic of Rough and Ready. Alas, when those same miners were denied the purchase of alcohol at a nearby town on the grounds that they were foreigners, the camp voted to rejoin the Union in time to celebrate Independence Day.

Unfortunately for storytellers and students of history, the facts only muddy the above legend's waters. The Foreign Miners Tax is the likely candidate for the onerous assessment in question. However, it was aimed at Chinese and Mexicans rather than "Americans." The bill was signed into law on April 13, 1850 (six days after secession) and did not become effective until June 1. As for the question of statehood, California Territory would not enter the Union as a free and undivided State until September 9, 1850 (over five months after secession).

Some versions of the story state that Rough and Ready did not rejoin the nation until July 1851 rather than 1850. Others claim that "hostilities" did not officially end until 1948, when the town requested a post office. An inconvenient point for that particular report is that a post office had been established in 1851 and has almost continuously served the local populace. One variation addresses this by stating that the residents wanted their post office reopened after it had closed during the Second World War and that the process of rejoining the Union in 1948 was merely a matter of making it official on the part of the federal government.

Convoluted as the various versions are, however, none preclude the possibility that some truth lies at the story's heart. After all, rumors and hearsay had exaggerated effects in isolated communities. A resolution of secession may very well have passed based on incomplete and distorted facts. Decades of folklore would have taken it from there.

HENRY PLUMMER AND THE VIGILANCE COMMITTEE

No collection of tales about the Old West would be complete without at least one illustrating what sometimes passed for law and order on the frontier.

In 1862, the cry of "Gold!" came from the southwest corner of what would become Montana Territory. The population that summer reached four hundred and reportedly grew to at least four thousand the following year. Criminal activity increased accordingly. And in the search for a sheriff, charismatic newcomer William Henry Plummer was elected to the post.

Henry Plummer

Historians are divided on the series of events that began in late 1863. Some say that a crime wave of at least one hundred murders and gold shipment robberies, perpetrated by a well-organized gang of road agents, swept through the area of Bannack and Alder Gulch. Others claim there were no more than four botched and unconnected incidents.

The historical record reveals that a Vigilance Committee acting outside the law was formed in December and proceeded to hunt down

Historical view of Virginia City, Montana, from Alder Gulch.

any suspected gang member. Over the next two months, twenty-one men were hanged, including the alleged ringleader and mastermind: Sheriff Plummer.

That some of the Vigilantes' victims were innocent has long been established; as to Plummer's involvement in a crime wave of questionable magnitude, however, there remains sharp disagreement. Those historians who argue that one hundred or more murders and robberies are a gross exaggeration believe that Plummer's intention to stop the lynchings had caused him to become a marked man.

On May 7, 1993, his case was argued posthumously in court. When the jury was evenly divided on the verdict, the judge declared a mistrial. Unfortunately for Henry Plummer, his exoneration arrived 129 years too late.

County courthouse turned hotel, Bannack State Park, Montana, 2009.

Virginia City, Montana, street view, 2009.

HELL WITH THE FIRES OUT

By necessity, storytelling with the primary purpose of entertainment exaggerates some facts and diminishes or eliminates others. As a result, versions of an oft-told legend can become irreconcilable over time on many key points. The ghost town of Stanton, Arizona, stood out as a textbook example of this outcome during script research for *Ghosts of the West: The End of the Bonanza Trail*.

Though the sequence was cut from the film for several reasons (including the one noted above), the following narrative initially outlined for the documentary includes many typical story elements. The reader should note, however, that great discrepancies exist as to dates, and significant disagreements over the veracity of many parts of the tale remain unresolved.

◆

Charles Stanton

Placer mining and a stage route gave rise to the community of Antelope Station, Arizona Territory. By the early 1870s, the area's growing prosperity began attracting less desirable elements. Many believe they arrived in the form of Charles P. Stanton and a gang of desperadoes led by Francisco Vega.

Amongst the town's primary businesses were a general store owned by G. H. Wilson and a station run by William Partridge. Bad blood existed between the two, but sources differ on whether the rivalry began when pigs raised by Wilson broke into and damaged property owned by Partridge or whether that was the final incident in an ongoing conflict. Stanton seized upon the opportunity, convincing Partridge of the lie that "the owner of the pigs" was out to get him.

Partridge took the threat at face value and, in Old West style, shot Wilson to death in the street. In the aftermath, Wilson's partner John Timmerman took over the store's operations, and Partridge's creditors turned the station over to Barney Martin.

When Antelope Station earned the establishment of a post office,

Stanton, as postmaster, promptly renamed the settlement "Stanton." With Vega's gang allegedly as his instrument, he targeted the businesses' new principals, Timmerman and Martin, along with anyone else who stood in his way.

On a trip to Wickenburg, Timmerman was robbed and murdered. Stanton immediately took ownership of the store, claiming the now-deceased partners had left it to him. Regardless of suspicion, no one dared challenge his assertion.

Eventually, only Barney Martin stood between Charles Stanton and total control of the town. In the summer of 1886, after years of violent harassment, the Martin family finally packed up and left for Phoenix. Their failure to arrive prompted a search; weeks later, the charred remains of their bodies and wagon were discovered off the stage road east of Seymour.

Stanton was arrested for complicity in the massacre, but whether from lack of evidence or fear of reprisal, he walked free. Unchallenged and seemingly untouchable, he then took what he wanted and did as he pleased. Later that year, an unfortunate Mexican girl became the focus of his unwanted attention. The girl's brother, seeking to avenge his family's honor, shot Stanton to death inside the store once belonging to Wilson and Timmerman.

Within a few years of his murder, the town bearing his name finally died.

THE PIRACY OF THE DENVER & RIO GRANDE RAILROAD

In Silver Cliff, Colorado, the 1878 discovery of horn silver at the grass roots had brought on the wild excitement that comes at the start of a boom.

In *Stampede to Timberline*, Muriel Sibell Wolle described how claims were worked so thoroughly that the surface silver was soon exhausted. When the frenzy died down, many miners drifted off; some remained and spent money they did not have; and others continued to work their claims by sinking shafts. By the following summer, enough rich lodes had been discovered that the rush was on again.

The town boomed and would soon become the third most populous city in the state after Denver and Leadville. In 1880, the Denver & Rio Grande Railroad began extending its line to serve the area's mines. The excitement in Silver Cliff did not last long, however, for the plans indicated that the tracks would not enter the town. Rather, they would stop a mile or so west of it.

Around the terminus, the company began selling land owned by its directors and established the competing town of Westcliffe. As a consequence, Silver Cliff was robbed of the benefits and prosperity that a railroad usually brought.

A City in Two States

In August 1860, three prospectors discovered rich paying ore east of the Sierra Nevada near the site of what would become the city of Aurora. All the elements that generally flock to a boomtown were not long in arriving as the population skyrocketed.

Nevada Territory was created just over six months after discovery on March 2, 1861. California believed the city to be in California and designated Aurora as the seat of the newly created Mono County in April. Nevada believed Aurora to be in Nevada and designated it as the seat of the newly created Esmeralda County in November.

In April 1862, one particularly remarkable individual arrived to try his hand at prospecting: Samuel Clemens. His stay lasted just six months; but in that short time, he and his partners became millionaires—until their claim to the Wide West Mine was jumped ten days after discovery. Despondent, Clemens turned to correspondence with Virginia City's *Territorial Enterprise* and soon began writing under the name of Mark Twain. The pseudonym was a nod to his time on the Mississippi and meant "two fathoms," a safe depth for the riverboats he piloted in his youth. He would go on to write about his experiences in the book *Roughing It*. (And while a great story, the bit about the mine should be viewed as entertaining fiction.)

The wild years got wilder with the formation of the San Francisco Stock Exchange in September 1862, and speculation in mining stocks grew frenzied. The following June, Nevada's territorial governor (again, believing Aurora to be in Nevada Territory) appointed Esmeralda County officials. Elections were held on September 2, the same day as elections for Mono County, California, officials. Two weeks later, on September 16, a survey team placed the city on the Nevada side of the border.

Aurora reached its peak in 1863, and a building boom swept the city. In the fall, two prominent brick structures were completed at opposite ends of the Pine Street business district. On the north side of Pine, west of the Antelope Street intersection, stood the three-story Merchants' Exchange Hotel, the city's largest and most luxurious lodging. On the south side of Pine, east of Antelope, Preble & Devoe's Hall opened with the Esmeralda County offices and courthouse, saloons, and other businesses as tenants.

While it may have seemed as if the flush times would last forever, their end would not be long coming, and the house of cards built partially on stock speculation would soon collapse.

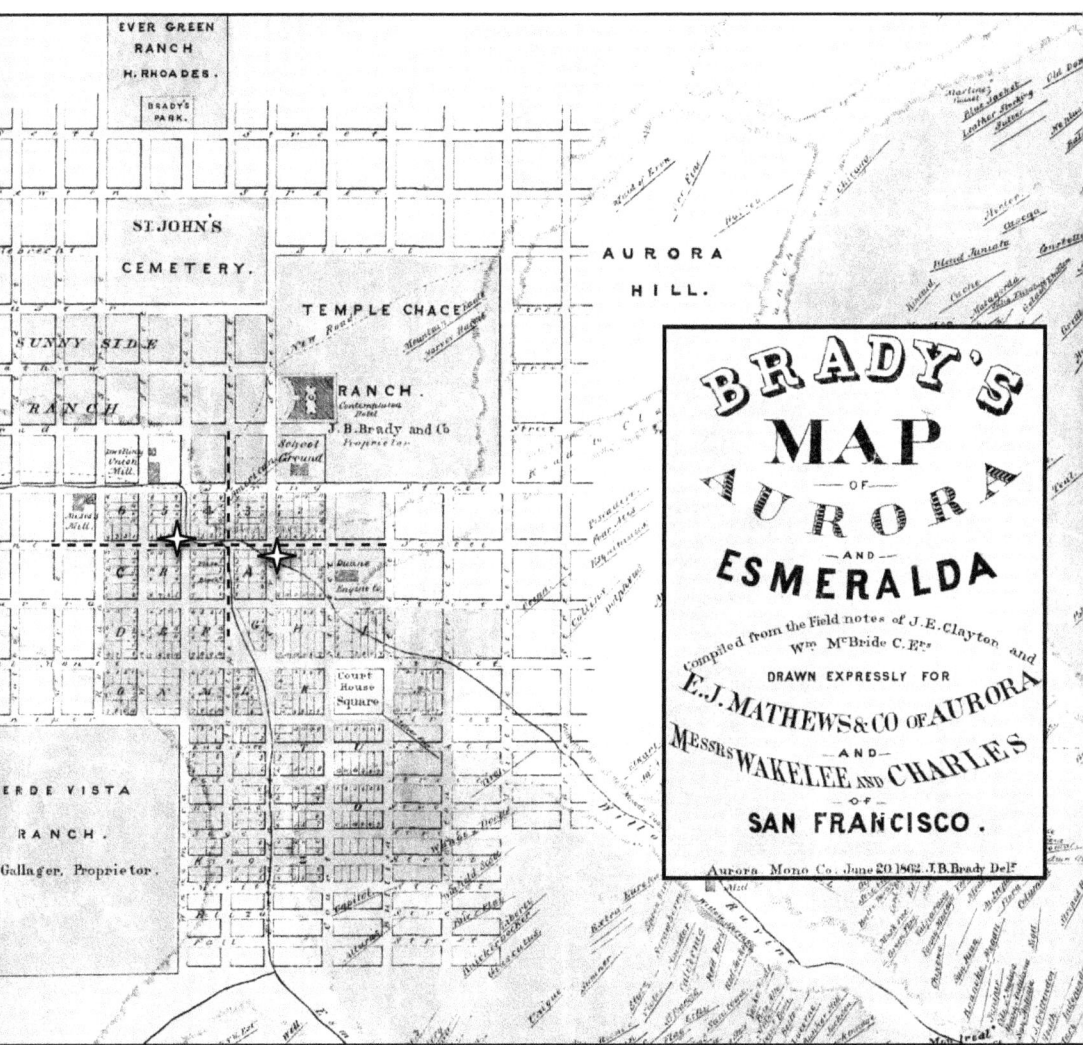

Extract from an 1862 map of Aurora. Note the legend refers to the city as "Aurora, Mono Co." The intersection of Antelope and Pine Streets is marked with dashed lines. The stars indicate the future locations of the Merchants' Exchange Hotel (left) and Preble & Devoe's Hall (right).

A Sea of Sin

"There are only two seasons in the region ... and these are, the breaking up of one Winter and the beginning of the next."
—Commentary on the Mono Lake area's weather cycle, often erroneously attributed to Bodie (about 10 miles north), Mark Twain, *Roughing It, 1872*

Bodie is becoming a quiet summer resort—no one killed here last week.
—Bodie's *The Daily Free Press*, June 1881

A sea of sin, lashed by the tempests of lust and passion...
—Reverend F. M. Warrington, 1881

"Good-by, God; we are going to Bodie in the morning."
—February 1879 article in Carson City's *Nevada Tribune* "quoting" a frightened 3-year-old girl whose family was moving to Bodie

"GOOD. By God we are going to Bodie in the morning."
—Traditional rebuttal attributed to the editor of an unknown Bodie newspaper who alleged that the little girl had been misquoted

◆

In 1859 W. S. Body and his companions found gold in the hills east of the Sierra Nevada, north of Mono Lake, California. During the winter of '59-'60, the prospector was caught in a blizzard on the way to his claim and froze to death. Discoveries to the northeast in Aurora and at the Comstock drew attention away from the site that would one day become

Bodie, California, shortly before its peak, circa 1880.
Main Street extends from center left to lower right.

the town of Bodie. But in 1876, a strike transformed the camp into a boomtown; further finds in 1878 added fuel to the fire.

It has been a common assumption in recent decades that during the wild years from 1877 through 1881, Bodie's population peaked somewhere between ten thousand and thirteen thousand. This number is likely a complete fabrication, often repeated rather than fact-checked. According to the U.S. Census of 1880, Bodie, Bridgeport, and Mill Creek Townships had a combined total of just 6,001, and all of Mono County came in at 7,499.

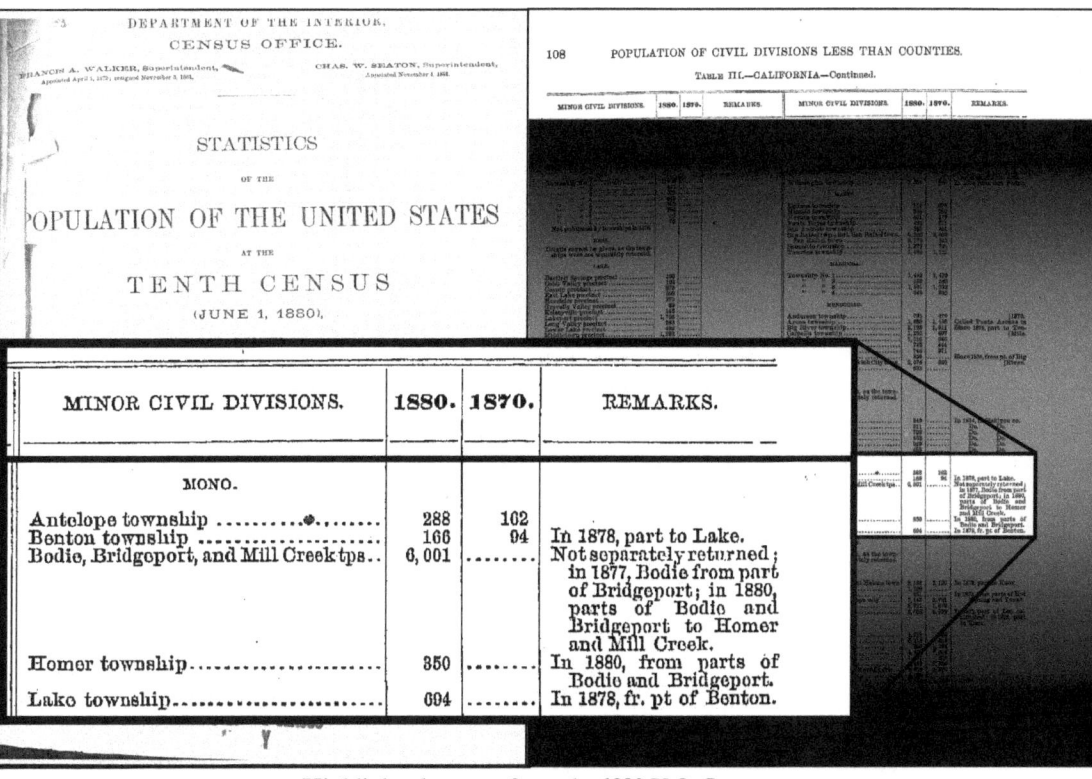

Highlighted extract from the 1880 U.S. Census.

Local papers of the time, which often advocated for their town, took issue with the breakout figure of 5,416 provided by the census enumerator. The *Daily Bodie Standard*, for instance, cited cases where some had not been counted and estimated the population nearer to seven thousand. While significant numbers of people were transient, and a mountain town could see large swings between winter and summer, it is highly improbable that Bodie had anywhere near ten to thirteen thousand residents, especially in light of the editorials in the papers of the day.

Daily Bodie Standard.

VOLUME III.   BODIE, MONO COUNTY, CALIFORNIA: THURSDAY, JULY 15, 1880.   NUMBER 179.

We have nine men in and about the STANDARD PRINTING HOUSE, but the Census Taker did not get the names of one of them that we know of. The same thing occured at one or two other places in town. It is believed that we have nearer to seven than five thousand.

THE BODIE CHRONICLE.

VOL. XIX.   BODIE, MONO COUNTY, CALIFORNIA, SATURDAY, JULY 17, 1880.   NO. 906.

ANOTHER GROWL—St. Louis and Chicago, San Francisco and Sacramento, have been growling because the census enumerators have not footed up a population equal to what has been claimed for them by their papers. And now comes Bodie a growling, the census taker giving us a population of only 5,417, when we have been claiming from 7,000 to 10,000 people in our altitudinous burg. Perhaps our enumerators have omitted a few, but is not 5,416 a goodly population for a place that may be said to be really only about two years old? We think it is.

Comments from the editors of two Bodie papers regarding the 1880 Census.

Regardless of the correct figure, Bodie was a true boomtown of the Old West. As shown in the street view below and from Standard Hill on page 24, Main Street became a mile-long stretch of one- and two-story frame buildings.

This image of Main Street in Bodie is believed to have been captured in 1877, making it the earliest known photograph of the town.

By the late 1880s, the wild years had ended, and the city had begun its inevitable decline. However, though a disastrous fire consumed sixty-four buildings on June 25, 1892, Bodie was not yet finished.

Electricity to run the stamp mill came to town toward the end of the year of the fire, and the introduction of the cyanide process in 1894 made old mines profitable once again. As those developments progressed, new structures arose on the sites of those that had burned. The United States Hotel pictured on the following page was one such addition. Its owners reportedly spared no expense in constructing high-quality, elegant lodging. Photos taken in later years show a second-story extension over the rooms to the left of the facade.

Top: An early view of the U.S. Hotel at the intersection of Main and Mill Streets.
Bottom: Guests watch a tug-of-war contest from the hotel's second-story balcony.

A Lady Called Silver Heels

Fiction is history that did not happen, and history is fiction that did.
—Unknown

A prime example of the above adage is the set of tales surrounding one of the earliest camps of the Pikes Peak gold rush founded in what was then Kansas Territory. Despite that there are few signs that the camp ever existed, Buckskin Joe, Colorado, remains a much-romanticized site to the present day.

The camp was first named Lauret (or Laurette), said to have been a shortened form of "Lauranette," a combination of the first names of the wives of two prominent brothers in the area. Other accounts assert that it was named after the sweetheart of discoverer Joseph Higganbottam. Regardless, the name did not stick with the miners, who referred to the settlement as Buckskin Joe.

This photo of Buckskin Joe is generally assumed to have been taken in 1864, some years after the region was partitioned from Kansas Territory.

The building thought to have been Tabor's Mercantile, Buckskin Joe, Colorado.

In its heyday, several thousand are claimed to have resided in the town, including the future Silver King, Horace Tabor, who arrived with his wife Augusta in 1861. Together they ran a mercantile and took in boarders; Horace also was the first postmaster.

Buckskin Joe held the Park County seat and boasted a newspaper, bank, dancing school, theaters, various stores, billiard halls, and a lively red-light district. There was also a hall where a beautiful, enigmatic young lady nicknamed Silver Heels danced.

Legend tells of a smallpox epidemic that swept the camp in the early 1860s, possibly 1861. Nearly all activity halted as residents shut themselves in, and pleas for assistance were sent as far away as Denver. The miners who succumbed lay sick and dying in their cabins; but full of compassion and unconcerned for her safety, Silver Heels visited and cared for the ill at her peril.

The hall where Silver Heels danced, circa 1940 (top) and 2021 (bottom).

When the plague left the camp, the surviving miners collected a purse of $5,000 to show their gratitude, but no answer came when they called to present it at her home. Her cabin was found vacant, and she was never seen again. Some speculated that she had been stricken by the disease, and it had robbed her of her beauty. In later years, stories were told about a heavily veiled woman seen weeping over the graves of the miners. Whenever the mourner was approached, she would dart away before anyone could catch a glimpse of her.

The markers on most early graves in the Buckskin Joe cemetery have long since deteriorated.

Some versions of the legend say the miners raised $4,000, and Colorado Senator Edward O. Wolcott added the other $1,000. But considering that these events were supposed to have occurred in the early 1860s, some major sticking points for this variation appear insurmountable: Colorado was not granted statehood until 1876, and Wolcott (born in 1848) did not move from Ohio to Colorado until 1875 nor become a Senator until 1889.

While embellishment of the purse details may be dismissed as the work of storytelling devices, verifying the main plot point of the epidemic is much more problematic. The cemetery would present a primary source of information on causes of death during the camp's heyday, but most of the early wooden markers long since have rotted away or bear inscriptions that have been indiscernible for the better part of a century.

That leaves the newspapers, where the appearance of smallpox was always of interest. During extensive research on the town, Park County historian and author Christie Wright found no mention of an outbreak or plea for help in the currently available historic Colorado newspapers published in the 1860s (visit ColoradoHistoricNewspapers.org for more information). A search by this book's author revealed notices of the disease amongst Union and Confederate troops in the east, cases in Denver and amongst the Cheyenne in the Territory, at least one apparent wish for something exciting on which to report when the news was dull, and similar instances but little else.

Appearing with regularity during that time were ads for stage lines, gold dust trade, and merchandise consignments, along with news about assays, toll roads, political visits, court sessions, and other daily events. There were even lengthy reports on the camp's articles of organization and how it received the name of Lauret. Reason would dictate, therefore, that reporting on an epidemic would be considerable. Yet, an article entitled "Reminiscences of Buckskin Joe" in the June 19, 1879 edition of

The original Park County courthouse, South Park City Museum, Fairplay, Colorado.

The Fairplay Flume contained no hint of the legend's drama (for additional information, see Appendix IV, pages 97-98).

Considering all the press noted above, it seems highly improbable that an outbreak, pleas for help, and fearless care by a mysterious woman would have gone without mention. While there may have been clues on vanished grave markers or coverage in long-lost local papers such as the *Buckskin Joe Mountaineer*, there sadly is no evidence today that a smallpox outbreak and the events that followed ever occurred in Buckskin Joe.

By 1868, the boom years had ended; the camp was nearly deserted; the Tabors had moved on to the Leadville area; and the county seat had been lost to Fairplay. It is said that Mount Silverheels, which stands to the northeast, was named in honor of the selfless dancehall girl.

Historical view of Buckskin Joe, Colorado, believed to have been taken in 1864, at about the same time as the photo on page 29.

In the twentieth century, the building believed to have been Tabor's store became part of the "Buckskin Joe" tourist attraction near Royal Gorge, about a two-hour drive south from Denver and which has since been purchased and moved to a private ranch owned by William Koch. However, the original courthouse building (see page 33) is preserved as part of the South Park City Museum in Fairplay, approximately seven road miles away; and the cemetery remains in use by the nearby town of Alma.

Other than the burial ground and the collapsed ruins of what some believe was the dancehall where Silver Heels performed, all that remains of the townsite today is an empty field and a haunting legend.

Site of Buckskin Joe as it appeared in 2015.

Above: Main Street in Marysville, Montana.
Below: Gillian Hall and Fraternity Hall in Elkhorn, Montana.

ACT THREE: BUST

Twenty-six whiskey hells and two Vigilance Committees graced those days of prosperity and mirthful gallows, of stock-board and the gay delirium of speculation. Now her sad streets are lined with closed doors; a painful silence broods over quartz mills, and through the whole deserted town one perceives that melancholy security of human life which is hereabouts one of the pathetic symptoms of bankruptcy. The "boys" have gone off to merrily shoot one another somewhere else, leaving poor Aurora in the hands of a sort of coroner's jury who gather nightly at the one saloon and hold dreary inquests over departed enterprise.
    —Clarence King, *Mountaineering in the Sierra Nevada*, 1871

Gold and silver created the towns, and the wealth those towns produced across the thousands of mining districts throughout the western Territories and States was truly staggering. For instance, gold taken from the gulches around Helena, Montana, amounted to more than twice what the U.S. had paid France for the entire Louisiana Territory. Colorado's Cripple Creek district produced $340 million in gold in just 25 years—based on a value of $16 to $18 per ounce. And in the Black Hills of the Sioux Nation, a discovery in 1876 would eventually stand above them all as one of the richest mines in the world (see "The Homestake" on page 44).

Yet regardless of the millions that had been generated, once the ore played out or larger economic forces came into play, much of the population left, and many of the towns faded from history or died.

The Panic of '93

The Sherman Silver Purchase Act had required the federal government to procure at market value and coin silver produced by domestic mines. When the Panic of '93 hit, the U.S. repealed the Act, sending the price of silver into a tailspin.

The news spread like wildfire through the western states. Freighters abandoned silver ore on the sides of trails and railroads, and entire towns in Montana and Colorado were nearly deserted within twenty-four hours. In Granite, Montana, the steam whistle at Granite Mountain Mining's mill was tied open the day after the repeal, announcing the shutdown of operations. Residents packed up what belongings they could bring with them and left town.

Granite, Montana, circa 1890. Miners' Union Hall is the large building near the top center.

Though dealt a severe blow, mining at the richest lodes remained profitable. As the price of silver recovered in the years after the crash, operations resumed at some abandoned workings.

Like many mining camps, Granite had more ups and downs in the decades that followed. But in the late 1950s, while a crew was assessing the old mine shafts, a fire that began in the surface engine room destroyed most of the town.

Miners' Union Day parade in Granite, Montana, circa 1890.

Above: Miners' Union Hall, Granite, Montana, 1965 (left) and 2009 (right).
Below: Street view with Miners' Union Hall in the background, 2009.

A Tale of Two Carsons

In 1882, a year after Christopher Carson staked out the Bonanza King mine, a camp bearing his name formed in the wilderness on the Atlantic side of the Continental Divide. Situated high above timberline, access for bringing supplies in and shipping ore out plagued the remote Colorado settlement for years. Some miners chose to stick close to their claims throughout the brutal winters; but when the federal government demonetized silver during the Panic of '93, Carson came to an end.

In 1896, the discovery of gold nearby revived the district, and another camp formed at a lower elevation on the Pacific side of the Divide. The new Carson thrived for a few years, then mining activity began its inevitable decline; people left for richer grounds; and in 1903, the post office finally closed.

Top: The remaining ruins of old Carson are quickly vanishing.

Right: Though vandalized, several standing structures at new Carson have been reroofed and stabilized.

The Fate of Silver Cliff

In just three years, Silver Cliff had grown from a single cabin into the third largest population center in Colorado with 5,040 residents, according to the U.S. Census.

Silver Cliff, Colorado, during the boom years, c. 1880-1885.

Boasting ten miles of streets, Silver Cliff issued bonds to build water works; but when the boom ended in the early 1880s, people drifted away. With a lower tax base, the city defaulted on its obligations. A new town council re-financed the debt, raising taxes to meet the payments. But to avoid them, residents moved their houses and shops down the road to Westcliffe, the town established by the Denver & Rio Grande.

Much of Silver Cliff was moved away, and today a visitor would be hard-pressed to find those ten miles of streets.

Top: Silver Cliff, Colorado, c. 1886-1887.
Bottom: Silver Cliff, Colorado, c. 1910-1915.

Dramatic changes are evident by comparing the photo on page 42 with the left half of the top photo and comparing the rightmost portion of the top image with the bottom.

THE HOMESTAKE

After George Armstrong Custer announced the presence of gold in the Black Hills in 1874, prospectors swarmed into Sioux Nation territory in violation of the 1868 Treaty of Fort Laramie. Wherever they found "the color," illegal camps like Deadwood formed near the workings (see pages 10 and 11).

Assayed at one ounce per ton, ore from the Homestake mine was considered low grade. However, it was the source of the placer gold in Deadwood and Whitewood Creeks, and the body of ore was large.

Located approximately three miles from Deadwood, the town of Lead quickly grew to support operations of several combined claims. According to U.S. Census data, it became the second most populous city in South Dakota by 1900.

By the time operations ceased in 2002, the mine had reached a depth of 8,240 feet. Over its 125 years of operation, it had produced nearly ten million ounces of silver and over forty million ounces of gold—an amount equal to approximately one-third of California's *entire* gold output during the second half of the nineteenth century.

Left: Panoramic view of the Homestake Mine's massive open pit in Lead, South Dakota.

Above: Headstone of Seth Bullock, first sheriff of Deadwood, in Mount Moriah Cemetery, Deadwood, South Dakota.

SUNSET FOR THE CITY OF THE DAWN

A gold mine is a hole in the ground with a liar at the top.
—Often attributed to Mark Twain (apocryphal)

An event in Aurora, Nevada Territory, 1864 (labeled as "Washington's Day celebration," as "February 1864," and as "Election Speeches," depending on the archive). The building in the foreground opened in October 1863 as Preble & Devoe's Hall and held the Esmeralda County offices.

Aurora was booming, but flush times never last forever. The photo above is believed to have been taken in February 1864. Shortly thereafter, the deposits so rich near the surface began giving out at a depth of about one hundred feet. A sell-off of mining stocks ensued, and the revelation that stock price manipulation had taken place only made the panicked selling more acute. Mills began to close, and the population plummeted to less than half by the summer, a season when it is usually on the rise.

West-facing view of Pine Street, Aurora, Nevada, 1866.

A year and a half later, the most destructive fire in Aurora's history destroyed a large portion of the commercial district on Antelope Street, and the population dropped still further. (In the above photo, most of the frame buildings at center- and upper-right behind the businesses facing Pine Street were consumed.) However, the city still held the county seat, and its remaining businesses thrived due to its proximity to nearby mining camps. The courthouse (Preble & Devoe's Hall) is on the left in these photos; the large building in the background on the opposite side of the street is the Merchants' Exchange Hotel.

West-facing view of Pine Street, Aurora, Nevada, early 1870s.

In 1877, mineral strikes just over the border in Bodie, California, revived interest in Aurora. A second boom began but ended abruptly in 1881 when pumps could no longer drain the Del Monte mine. The following year, an arsonist destroyed the Merchants' Exchange Hotel. Its burned-out shell would stand for the rest of Aurora's life, a tragic reminder of her past glory. The bad luck continued into 1883 when the county seat was lost to Hawthorne, the recently created railroad town and temporary terminus for the Carson and Colorado Railroad.

By 1890, less than one-fourth of the buildings present during the heyday remained. The post office, which had once stamped "Esmeralda, Cal" on mail pieces, closed in 1897. At the turn of the century, only a few dozen people still called Aurora "home."

Fortune seemed to return to the city in 1906. A new twenty-stamp mill began processing ore from mines recently acquired by James Stuart Cain of Bodie, California, and his associates. The population increased, and the post office reopened. Electric power was extended from Bodie in 1910, and telephone service arrived in 1913 as a new company began construction on what would be the second-largest stamp mill in Nevada. A final boom began, and in 1914 the population swelled to about three hundred fifty. Vacant buildings were refurbished, and the old county courthouse was converted into the Hotel Warren. It would become the Esmeralda Hotel the following year.

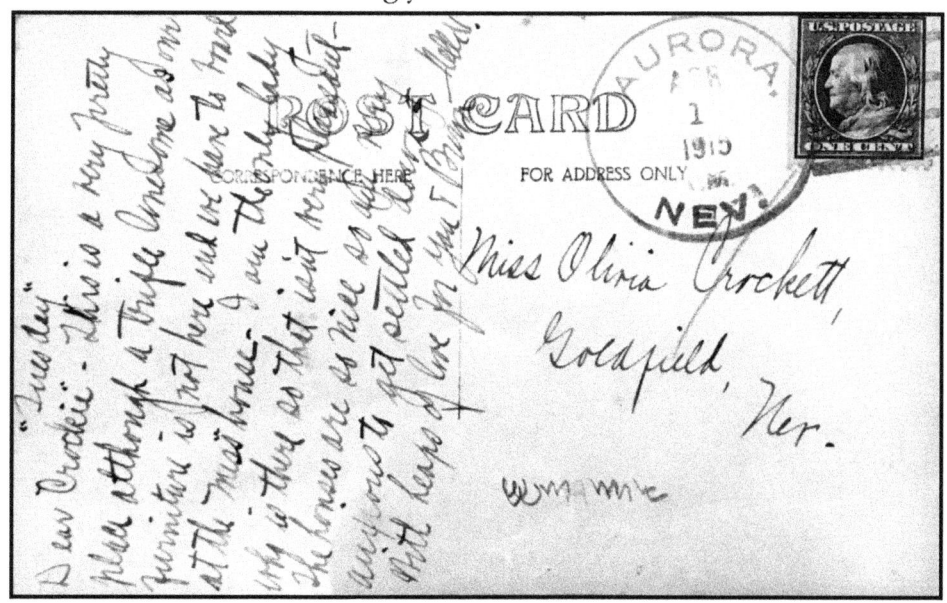

Postcard sent from "the only lady" in Aurora, Nevada, during the final boom.

East-facing view of Pine Street, Aurora, Nevada, circa 1913.

Independence Day celebration at Hotel Warren, Aurora, Nevada, 1914.

East-facing view of Pine Street during Aurora's Independence Day celebration, 1914.

By 1916 however, the quantity and quality of ore arriving at the mill had begun to decline. When the U.S. entered the Great War in 1917, labor and materials for processing became scarce, and their costs increased. Aurora celebrated its last Independence Day in 1917, and the public school concluded its last full academic year in June 1918. The mine and mill closed the following October. By January 1919, Aurora's hundreds had dwindled to less than twenty. Communication with the outside had ceased, and the stage no longer ran. On May 31 of that year, the post office closed for the final time, and the remaining residents had to travel to Hawthorne for mail.

Views of Rhyolite, Nevada: The long-abandoned Las Vegas and Tonopah Railroad station (above) and the ruins of the John S Cook & Co. Bank (below).

ACT FOUR: GHOST

I knew the wild riders and the vacant land were about to vanish forever, and the more I considered the subject, the bigger the Forever loomed.
—Frederic Remington

The fates of the camps varied considerably after progressing from discovery to boom to bust. As in the case of Silver Cliff, some are still occupied but are shadows of what they once were. Others have vanished with barely a trace, like Buckskin Joe, or stand in skeletal ruin like Rhyolite, Nevada. Only a lucky few, such as Bannack and Coloma, are protected and preserved by nearby locals, historical societies, and the States. The two tales in this chapter serve to illustrate the extremes.

A Sea of Fire

By 1910 Bodie's population had fallen to 698, according to U.S. Census data, representing as little as ten percent of the multitudes that had swarmed its streets during the late 1870s and early 1880s. As would happen with Aurora across the state line, the mines began to fail over the next half-decade, and many closed. The railroad was abandoned in 1917 and sold for scrap the following year.

When an article in an outside newspaper referred to Bodie as the best ghost town to visit, tourists and souvenir hunters began arriving, reportedly showing little respect for property that was not their own. Some residents later recalled dinners being interrupted by strangers who had walked into their homes on the assumption that they were exploring (or ransacking) an empty town.

On June 23, 1932, smoke began rising from a building behind the Sawdust Corner Saloon at the southwest corner of Union and Main streets. The first men and women drawn to the scene by the signs of fire soon discovered that the waterworks were clogged with debris due to a lack of maintenance over the years.

Unhindered, the blaze spread rapidly along the west side of Main. Wind generated by the growing conflagration carried sparks and burning embers into the air, igniting buildings on the opposite side of the thoroughfare. The old wooden structures burst into flame, and residents could do little more than helplessly watch their town die.

Within ninety minutes, most of Bodie was gone; it was later determined that a two-and-a-half-year-old boy playing with matches had caused the destruction. From its heyday half a century earlier, it is estimated that only five to ten percent of the buildings remained after the great fire. The extent of the devastation is illustrated in the following four sets of photographs.

Bodie Then & Now: west side of Main Street north across Green Street intersection, c. 1910s (top) and from a slightly different angle in 2019 (bottom).

Bodie Then & Now: south-facing view of Main Street, south of the intersection with Union, c. 1910s (top) and 2015 (bottom).

Bodie Then & Now: east side of Main Street south of the Union intersection, circa 1910 (top) and 2015 (bottom). The U.S. Hotel stands at the far left in the top photo. From this vantage point, the business block in the top image would have concealed the sight of the mill seen clearly in the bottom photo.

Bodie Then & Now: town as seen from Standard Hill, circa 1880 (top); shortly after the 1932 fire (middle); and as a California State Historic Park, 2015 (bottom).

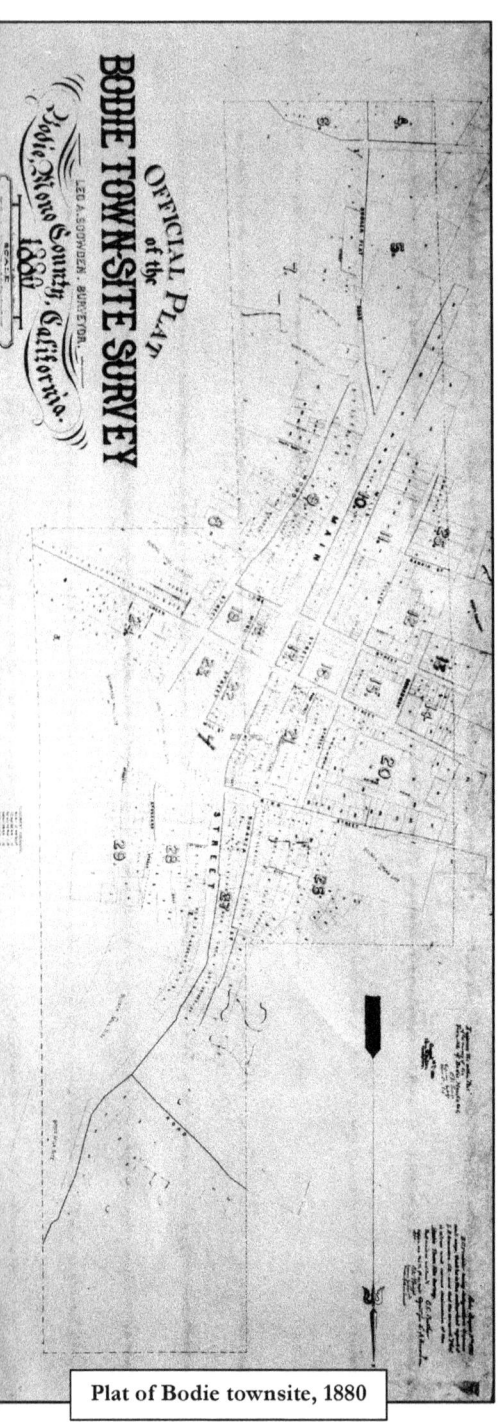

Plat of Bodie townsite, 1880

Twenty-five-year-old James Stuart Cain had arrived in Bodie in 1879. As both Bodie and nearby Aurora declined, he purchased properties and claims. When the 1932 fire hit, Cain suffered the most significant losses. Not long after, he hired caretakers to protect what survived and moved to San Francisco to live with his daughter and son-in-law. He passed away in 1936, leaving his heirs with title to much of the townsite.

In 1942 the War Production Board issued Limitation Order L-208, requiring nonessential mining activity to cease. The post office closed the same year. Following the Second World War, camping, exploration, scavenging, and vandalism increased despite the caretakers.

In 1958, the Cain family approached the State of California about preserving Bodie. Despite the objections of other families who still owned property in town, the state purchased the site and opened Bodie State Historic Park to the public a few years later.

California Department of Parks and Recreation keeps the town in a state of arrested decay. There is no restoration—only maintenance and repairs. Entry by the public into most buildings is restricted so that all remains as it was when acquired. Nothing is moved, and not even the dust is disturbed. The result is the largest unrestored ghost town in the United States.

Without question, it is one of the best to visit.

Top: East-facing view of Green Street from Park Street, Bodie State Historic Park, California.

Bottom: Northwest view of the town from the intersection of Wood and Green Streets, Bodie State Historic Park, California.

Solitary structures with impressive views in Bodie State Historic Park, California.

Swazey Hotel (top); Dechambeau Hotel and I.O.O.F. Hall (bottom), Bodie State Historic Park, California.

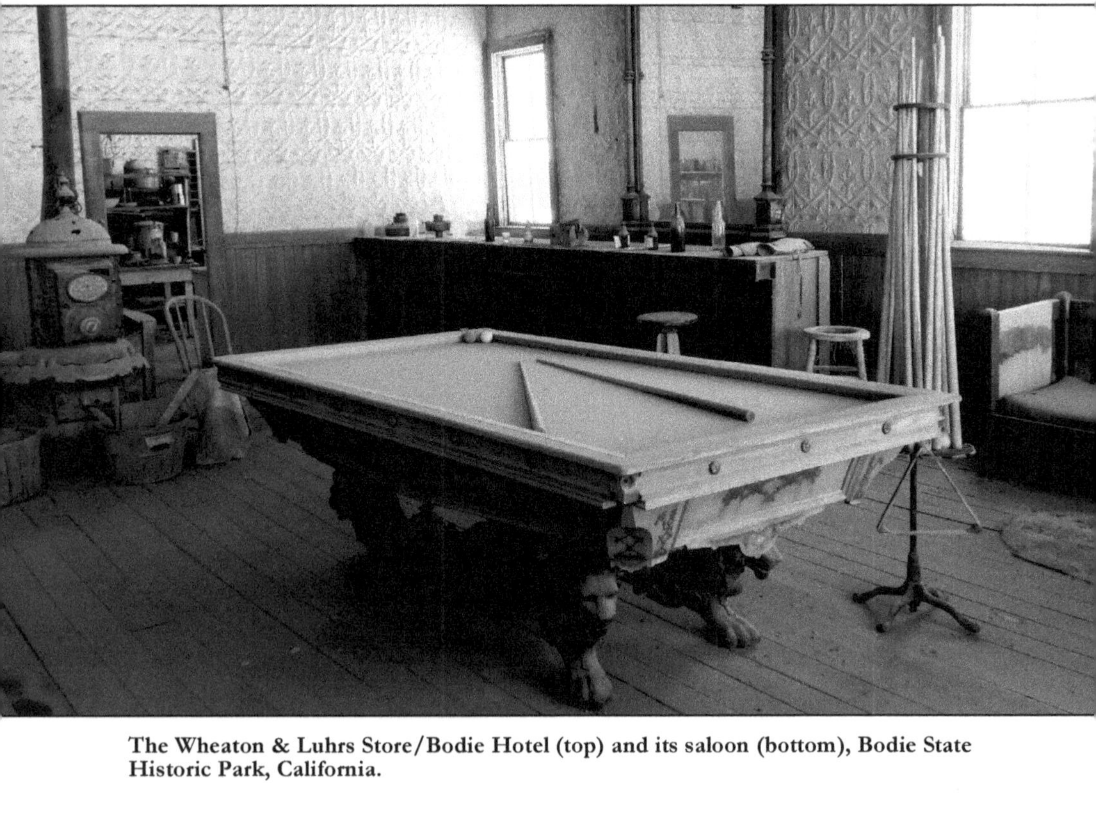

The Wheaton & Luhrs Store/Bodie Hotel (top) and its saloon (bottom), Bodie State Historic Park, California.

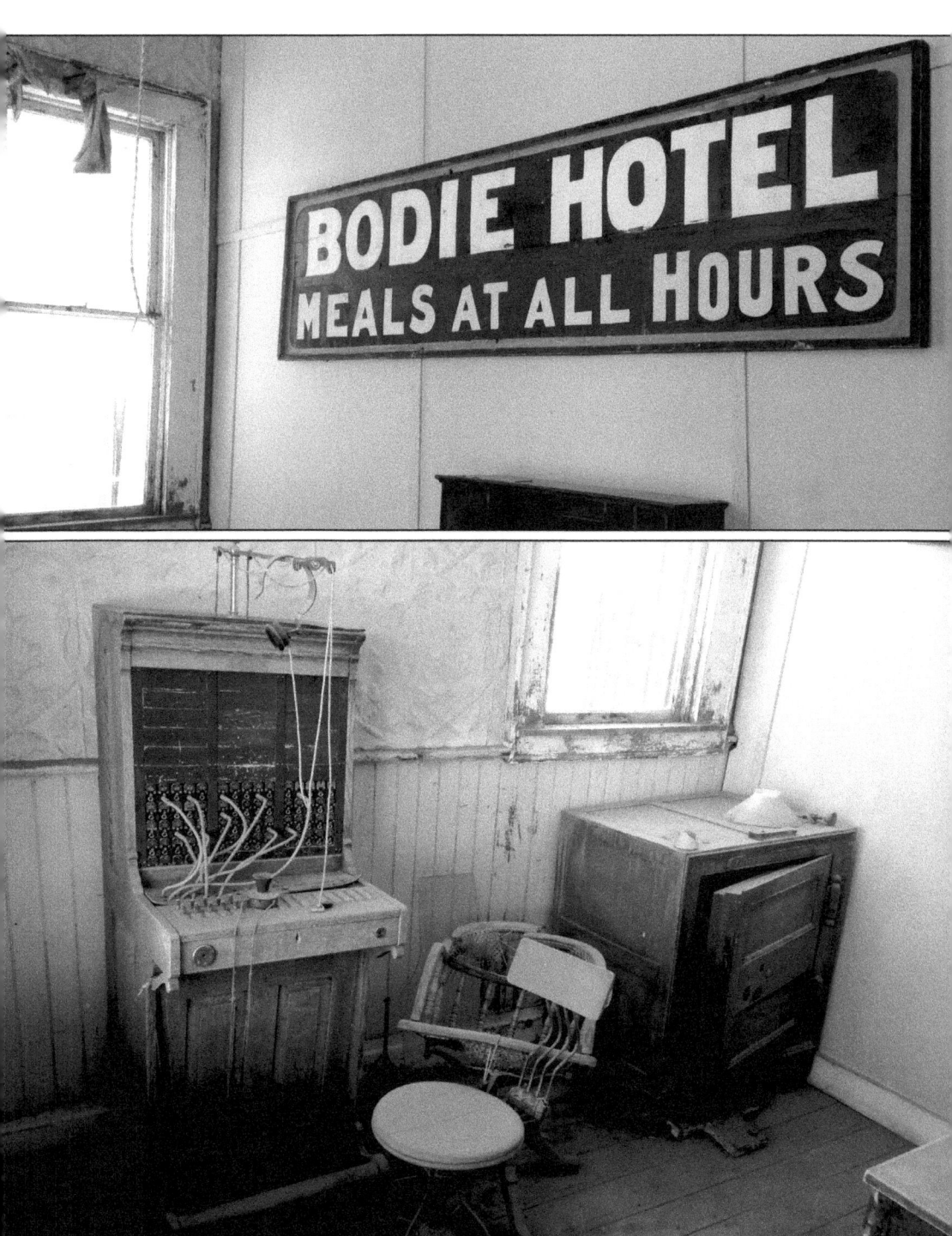
Bodie Hotel sign (top) and telephone switchboard (bottom) inside hotel office, Bodie State Historic Park, California.

Interior of Sam Leon's bar, Bodie State Historic Park, California.

Interior of Lottie Johl's residence, Bodie State Historic Park, California.

Boone Mercantile and Warehouse, Bodie State Historic Park, California.

Classroom in the schoolhouse (top); Methodist Church (bottom), Bodie State Historic Park, California.

Headstone of James B. Perry, Bodie State Historic Park, California.

NIGHTFALL FOR THE CITY OF THE DAWN

Across the border in Nevada, Bodie's sister city, where Samuel Clemens got a taste of the West, was much less fortunate. After fires and a quarter century of near-abandonment, less than twenty-five percent of Aurora's buildings remained when the photo below was taken. The view is roughly to the east-southeast. Pine Street runs through the town from the upper left at the base of the hills to the bottom center right of the image. Antelope Street is the major road extending from the left and intersecting Pine in the middle of the downtown business district. (Refer to the city map on page 23.)

Aurora, Nevada, looking southeast from Lover's Leap, circa 1890.

From the vantage point in the photo above, the three-story building in the foreground on the north side of Pine is the Merchants' Exchange Hotel, which had opened in the fall of 1863 and was destroyed by arson less than twenty years later. The two-story building with the balcony in the background on the south side of Pine is the old county courthouse, which ended its days as the Esmeralda Hotel.

Independence Day celebration at the Esmeralda Hotel, Aurora, Nevada, c. 1914-1915.

Above is a closer view of the Esmeralda taken at an Independence Day celebration during the revival years. But as noted in Chapter Three, the final boom was the last hurrah for Nevada's City of the Dawn. The photo below was taken approximately ten years later. Note the dramatic change in the condition of the street and the decay of the Esmeralda and surrounding buildings.

East-facing view of Pine Street and the Esmeralda Hotel, circa 1925.

In 1924, a cabin thought to have been one in which Mark Twain lived was moved from Aurora to a park in Reno "to preserve it."

The 1920s and '30s saw Aurora as the kind of ghost town that many conjure in their imaginations when they hear the term; but by the early 1940s, the city was rapidly succumbing to the elements and souvenir hunters. In her book *Ghosts of the Glory Trail,* author-explorer Nell Murbarger wrote of a weeklong visit shortly after the Second World War. She described the city as being full of vacant buildings, still furnished, and that an entire rail car would be insufficient to hold the museum-quality items that could be gathered.

"Mark Twain's cabin" in Aurora, Nevada.

However, even before Murbarger's time there, brick salvage operations had begun; and while some of the buildings were sold for that purpose, none escaped dismantling in the end. The photo at left was taken perhaps two years after her trip. Sagebrush has all but reclaimed Pine Street; the Esmeralda hotel, which stood on the east end of the thoroughfare, has been reduced to an indistinguishable, single-story shell when viewed from the west end of the road. The three photos on pages 70 and 71 illustrate the destruction of the historic city.

East-facing view of Pine Street, circa 1950. The Merchants' Exchange Hotel is on the left.

West-facing view of Pine Street, circa 1913.

As seen from the opposite end of the street in the photo above, the Esmeralda stands in the foreground on the left while looking west down Pine towards Lover's Leap (the bluff at upper right). Perhaps less than fifty people remained in the one-time city of five thousand when the photo was taken.

West-facing view of Pine Street, 1934.

The photo above was captured from a similar vantage point just over twenty years later. The Esmeralda's balcony has long since collapsed, and many wooden structures are gone. Salvaging and wholesale theft of the town would soon begin, and it would not take long.

Where Samuel Clemens got his first taste of a western mining camp—where once stood a city of a thousand buildings—only rotting boards, shards of glass, and broken bricks remain today. And in that park in Reno, vandals and souvenir hunters had utterly destroyed Mark Twain's cabin before the last of Aurora's structures had vanished from her deserted streets.

West-facing view of Pine Street, 2015.

Had a small boy not been playing with matches in Bodie and had some old timers of abandoned Aurora held on long enough for a preservation movement to begin, it seems more than likely that Bodie, California, and Aurora, Nevada, would have stood as the most spectacular historic district of the old American West.

Alas, it is one we are fated to visit only in our imaginations.

Now part of Mineral County, Aurora's cemetery stands alone as a reminder of the city that once flourished in the valley below. The isolated burial ground has suffered horrific vandalism, prompting the erection of the sign in the above photograph.

Judge William M. Boring, Nevada State Senator, is buried here (opposite page, top). Amongst the unmarked graves rest veterans of the War of 1812 and the Mexican-American War, along with soldiers from the Union and Confederate armies of the Civil War (opposite page, bottom).

In Honor
of Their Service to the Nation

These U.S. military veterans died and were buried in the Aurora
Cemetery. The locations of their graves are unknown and unmarked.

Civil War

Samuel R. Avery, USA
Romilly E. Foote, CSA
Ira P. Hale, Calif Vol
John Hawkins, Calif Vol

W.T. Lawrence, USA
Sylvester E. Light, USA
James M. Meredith, Calif Vol
Roderick D. Smith, Calif Vol

Mexican War
William Henry Hall, USA

War of 1812
Dennis Biggs, Tenn Vol

Erected by the Citizens and Board of Commissioners of Mineral County
with the cooperation of the U.S. Forest Service, as part of
The Nevada 150 Legacy Project for Nevada's Sesquicentennial (1864-2014)

"Wide West Mining Co. 1862" is engraved on this stone relic, salvaged from the ruins of Aurora. It is embedded in the ground beside a Bodie boardwalk.

ACT FIVE: LOST

As mentioned at the start, prospectors loved a good story, and tales often grew in the telling. While this is true of mines and placers discovered by sheer accident, it also applies to accounts of hidden caches buried by their owners and diggings that were sometimes lost almost as soon as they were found. In one legend, the discoverers remained unaware of the riches they had stumbled upon until it was too late.

THE LOST BLUE BUCKET PLACERS

In 1845 well before gold fever gripped the nation, young members of an Oregon-bound wagon train amused themselves with some shiny pebbles found alongside a stream. The children stored them beneath one of the wagons in a blue bucket, later lost on the journey.

An alternate version contends that some men used those stones as weights for their fishing lines. Believing they were mere copper, the pioneers discarded them along with a blue bucket after finishing their task.

Still another variation holds that hostile Indians drove the party to hide inside a cave. Only afterward was it realized that their sanctuary had been, in fact, an old mine tunnel.

Regardless of how they had been found, the pebbles that either remained as souvenirs in children's pockets or as recollections of an arduous journey were finally identified as gold after the strike at Sutter's Mill. The hunt then began in earnest for the Blue Bucket Mine.

THE CRYPTOGRAM AND THE HIDDEN CACHE

By some accounts, this next legend seems to have a firmer foundation in reality, even to the point where some evidence for it once existed.

Despite taking Indian trails to avoid notice, two prospectors transporting their gold from Montana Territory to the States were attacked by thieves not far from the Wyoming border. After his partner was killed, the panicked survivor filled a boot with as much of their treasure as it would hold, then buried it and hid until the robbers left.

Afraid to continue the journey with the gold, he carved a cryptogram on a nearby tree to guide him when he returned. But he never did. And though relatives and others have studied the cryptogram, none ever found the hidden cache—or reported having done so.

◆

Treasure and Tragedy on Slate Mountain

A tragic loss might follow closely on the heels of a rich find. While traveling to California in 1849, a group of prospectors found color in a streambed eight days' journey from Pike's Peak. Six of that original party stayed and dug for weeks, eventually striking high-grade ore. They had cached an estimated $100,000 of gold in a drift when provisions ran low and a snowstorm closed in. One of their number set out for supplies, but additional storms delayed his return. When he finally made his way back to the camp, he found the landscape radically transformed.

An avalanche and earth slide had torn their way down into the valley, taking with them the cabins and the men and burying beneath massive heaps of rubble the drift in which the gold had been stored. Broken by the tragedy, he did not speak of it again until 1881, when he relayed the tale just before passing away.

Ten years later, a prospector confided in a potential partner that he possessed the notebook of that ill-fated party's sole survivor, as well as the precise location of the cache and diggings.

The partner was skeptical until he saw samples of the ore. But two weeks later, the prospector was killed in a saloon brawl, and all knowledge of the mine was lost again.

◆

The Lost Dutchman Mine

Perhaps the greatest legend of all is the Lost Dutchman Mine in the Superstition Mountains of Arizona. Countless volumes have been written about it, many in direct contradiction with each other. So numerous are the inconsistencies and variations, and so many are the fictional tales and unrelated incidents inextricably woven as facts into the history, that some claim the mine never existed.

The Superstition Mountains of Arizona.

While many accounts begin with Coronado in the sixteenth century, most start with expeditions into the area by Don Miguel Peralta in the mid-1800s. According to legend, large quantities of gold were mined and cached nearby; over several trips, only a portion of that fortune was packed out for the return to Mexico. Resentful of the intrusion, the Apache attacked and slaughtered what would be Peralta's final undertaking at the western end of the mountains. The fleeing survivors abandoned the workings for good.

Years later, in the 1870s, a German immigrant named Jacob Waltz (and possibly a similarly named but ill-fated partner) discovered the mine and cache. Aware that his use of gold for currency had attracted attention and that his every move was being watched, it became increasingly difficult for Waltz to make the perilous trip from Phoenix, especially as old age and failing health overtook him.

He died in 1891 after revealing the mine's location to his deathbed caregiver Julia Thomas. The first search party headed into the Superstition Wilderness the following year, but accurate notes had not been taken, and the mine proved elusive.

Weavers Needle is an oft-mentioned landmark in Dutchman lore.

In the decades that followed, treasure hunters disappeared, committed suicide, and were brutally murdered. Any whose good fortune it was to find the mine or even get close to discovering its location seemed to have their luck run out.

However, the lure of a lost mine worth millions can be too great to resist. At one time, it was estimated that as many as eight thousand people each year made some effort to find it. Even today, many dedicate their lives to the search.

Over a century later, the legend continues to fire the imagination, and (perhaps) a mine of incredible wealth remains hidden.

A lone rider in the Superstition Wilderness, Arizona.

AFTERWORD

It was a driving, vigorous, restless population in those days. It was a curious population. It was the only population of the kind that the world has ever seen gathered together, and it is not likely that the world will ever see its like again.

—Mark Twain, *Roughing It*, 1872

Let us return to the question posed in the Introduction: *What is it about ghost towns that fascinates us?*

Quite possibly, the reasons for their allure are personal and vary from individual to individual. To some, the ghost towns may be a tangible representation of the Old West: of the storied population of which Mark Twain wrote and of the history they forged beyond the vast and vanished frontier.

Others may find that the remains of the towns and camps resonate with them on a more intimate level. At times it may seem as if the sites are not wholly forsaken but are yet haunted by the ghosts of the past: of those who suffered through unimaginable trials and hardships and who brought with them into the wilderness their hopes, dreams, fears, and failings.

> *Up to and including 1880 the country had a frontier of settlement, but at present the unsettled area has been so broken into isolated bodies of settlement that there can hardly be said to be a frontier line. In the discussion of its extent and westward movement it can not, therefore, any longer have a place in the census reports.*
>
> —Robert P. Porter, Henry Gannett, and William C. Hunt
> "Progress of the Nation: 1790 to 1890"
> *Report on Population of the United States at the Eleventh Census: 1890*

There is a palpable sense of loss holding the silent places of the West in a shroud. Disquietude lingers amongst the abandoned and vanished buildings. And beneath it all rest the ghosts of those who had occupied these lands long before the Spanish or Americans came to permanently alter the continent.

Frederic Remington saw "the Forever" looming. The Superintendent for the 1890 Census declared the frontier closed. And in 1913, Theodore Roosevelt wrote that: "that land of the West has gone now, 'gone, gone with lost Atlantis,' gone to the isle of ghosts and of strange dead memories."

More than a century has passed since those individuals witnessed the disappearance of the Old West, and its last vestiges are fast succumbing to the elements and its heedless inheritors. But the westward road beckons us still, and those "strange dead memories" continue to fascinate, intrigue, and even haunt us.

APPENDICES

I:
Summitville, Bodie, and the Homestake Mine

The individual stories of Summitville, Colorado, and Bodie, California, are often told without any mention of the other. After all, one is relatively obscure while the other is world-famous, and vast distances separate the San Juans of Colorado from the Sierra Nevada of California. But the fates of the two became perilously intertwined in the late twentieth century.

◆

The first placer gold was discovered around what would become Summitville, Colorado Territory, in 1870. As in Bodie, California, all remained relatively quiet until rich lodes were found to spark the stampede. But by the early 1890s, the town's glory years were in the past, and it stood as a ghost in the high country.

Boarding house in Summitville, Colorado.

During the twentieth century, the site saw operations continue on and off as new deposits were discovered or technological advances made the extraction of low-grade ore profitable. One such technique, known as cyanide heap-leaching, could result in recovery rates of up to ninety-seven percent of the gold value by treating the ore with cyanide and chemical solutions.

A cabin in Summitville, Colorado.

In 1986, Summitville Consolidated Mining Company, a wholly owned subsidiary of Vancouver-based Galactic Resources, Ltd, began open pit mining using cyanide heap-leaching for recovery. Within days, environmental concerns became evident when leaks in the heap pad liner were detected.

The same year, Homestake Mining Company surveyed its interests of over forty-seven square miles of property in the Bodie area, generating an internal report that indicated the presence of vast gold reserves. In 1987 the company offered the property for sale with open pit mining as the suggested extraction method (see photo on page 44).

Galactic purchased Homestake's interest in the Bodie district for approximately $39.5 million in 1988 and created Bodie Consolidated Mining Company as a wholly owned subsidiary.

On June 9, 1990, a fish kill was reported at a farm pond that had taken water from the Terrace Reservoir, eighteen miles downstream from the Summitville mine. In July, the Colorado Department of Wildlife's inventory of the reservoir's stocked fish population indicated a complete loss.

Around the same time, anonymous telephone calls notified the

Environmental Protection Agency that the mining company had been discharging untreated water into the Alamosa River. The EPA inspected the site in September, and Colorado began enforcement action the following year. Spills continued until operations ended in October 1991. Galactic announced it would sell nearly all its assets, including Bodie Consolidated Mining, to pay for the cleanup. The initial asking price for the latter was $35 million.

In October 1992, the California Department of Parks and Recreation entered into discussions with Galactic regarding the Bodie holdings, but even the reduced $12 million price tag remained beyond the department's means. The company stated it would market the property to other mining concerns if the state did not purchase it.

Part of the cleanup operations at the Summitville superfund site.

Summitville Consolidated Mining Company filed for bankruptcy in December, asserting it could not reclaim the site according to settlement agreements with the State of Colorado. It abandoned Summitville eleven days later. The EPA and the Colorado Department of Public Health and

Environment immediately took charge of the cleanup.

Galactic Resources filed for bankruptcy in Canada in January 1993, and control of its assets was turned over to a trustee. Without another buyer, negotiations between the trustee and California continued for several years.

After years of growing concern at the state and local level, the U.S. Congress passed the Bodie Protection Act of 1994 in October of that year, preserving 6,135 acres of federal land from further mineral exploitation. Deliberation and consideration of the Act and the activism leading up to its passage may have contributed to the disinterest of other mining companies in acquiring the Bodie claims, also helping drive the price downward.

By 1996, the asking price for the Bodie property had dropped to approximately $5 million. The following year, California purchased Bodie Consolidated Mining's records and property, which included 517 acres of land around the historic townsite. Bodie State Historic Park was rededicated that September.

As of 2018, taxpayers continue to fund the remediation of Summitville. In 2021, the EPA is expected to turn the site over to the State of Colorado, which will continue water runoff treatment at an expected annual cost of $2 million in perpetuity.

II:
BODIE, CALIFORNIA: JULY 4, 1880

The following account of Bodie's 1880 Independence Day celebration appeared in the *Daily Bodie Standard* on July 6, 1880.

THE CELEBRATION IN BODIE.

The Grandest Ever Witnessed in any Mining Camp---Unbounded Enthusiasm --- Nothing to Mar the Harmony of the Occasion--- A Grand Success in Every Particular.

The many guns fired from the many elevated stand-points, the preparations entered upon several days previous to the time for the celebration of our One Hundred and Fourth Anniversary, gave every evidence that Bodie was not to be behind any camp or town in the observance of this grand old natal day. Such enthusiasm, good feeling among the people generally, as goes to make a success of anything of public importance, never before was exhibited. Scarcely a society, civic or otherwise, but was represented.

The Miners' Union

Turned out two hundred and fourteen strong, under President Shaughnessy, and acted as the Guard of Honor to the Car of State. After what had transpired, the level-headed men of the Union are deserving of the many encomiums showered upon them. Let a veil be drawn over what has heretofore occurred. A lesson has been inculcated, and one which should never be forgotten, and the Miners' Union will henceforth occupy the position in our socialism to which its importance entitles it, if conducted upon the true principles it was organized to subserve—that of mutual benefit to its members, without entering into politics, religion or communistic ideas.

During Sunday Night

The firing of guns, anvils and giant powder showed the exceeding desire of our people to anticipate the grand celebration of our National Anniversary, and but few of them expected so great success to attend the efforts of the gentlemen and ladies composing the different committees, who labored indefatigably to fulfill their different stations. There are so many entitled to credit that it seems almost invidious to even attempt to speak of any particular individual or committee. But a true report cannot be given without going into detail, and, first of all, entitled to special mention, are the ladies who had charge of the decoration of the

Car of State,

Which, in its elaborateness, compared favorably with any we have ever seen in San Francisco or the Eastern cities. For three long days Mrs. Dr. Deal, Mrs. Hinkle, Mrs. Molinelli and Mrs. Harris worked with a will upon the car in its decoration, the preparation of the caps for the girls, rosettes for the horses, etc., and although almost tired out, they were liberally rewarded on yesterday morning to see as sweet a

Bevy of Little Beauties

As ever graced a Car of State in any section of the world. Following are names of the girls representing the different States and Territories: Goddess of Liberty, May Temple; Justice, Bertha Said; Pennsylvania, Delia Kingsley; Maryland, Ada Herrington; Connecticut, Oro Davison; Rhode Island, Maud Davison; Massachusetts, Cora McKinney; Vermont, Maud Sargentson; Delaware, Bessie Richards; New Jersey,

---

The images on pages 89 through 94 originally appeared as two-and-a-half columns of a seven-column page and were digitally arranged to fit the pages of this book.

Mabelle Wallace; Illinois, Clara Brainard; Indiana, Daisy Ogden; Kentucky, Clara Penrose; North Carolina, Katie Acquilarius; South Carolina, Alice Parsons; Georgia, Grace Morgan; Alabama, Gussie Elliott; Virginia, Alice Irwin; Idaho, Lida Pixley; Missouri, Clara Richardson; Arkansas, Belle McCrea; Tennessee, Clara Chapman; Kansas, Josie Kelley; Louisiana, Lillie Micomber; Minnesota, May Cross; Maine, Frankie Lynch; Wisconsin, Maggie Edwards; Nebraska, Lizzie Helmes; West Virginia, Maggie Loynahan; Colorado, Belle Martin; Indian Territory, Nellie Falkingham; Arizona, Lulu Barlow; Washington Territory, Cadie Kingsley; Montana Territory, Agnes Hector; Iowa, Ella Waldruff; New Hampshire, Lizzie Whitman; Oregon, Rosa Fisher; Alaska, Gussie Craft; Wyoming, Emma Bennett; Texas, Lizzie Taylor; Nevada, Annie Cochran; California, Rachel Dunn; District of Columbia, Minnie McGraw; Dakota, Elsie McGraw; Lower California, Annie Shaughnessy; Utah, Minnie Perry; Mississippi, Bell Allen; Ohio, Julia Allen; Michigan, Flora Sinclare; "Our Whole Country, Annie McGraw.

The Car of State was drawn by the splendid black six-horse team of J. Marden (who kindly donated the use of the team,) under the directing hand of Mr. Webber, and not an accident occurred, or anything to get up a scare among the little ones. Early in the evening Captain I. G. Messee and his efficient Aids were to be seen upon Main street, reconnoitering the ground for the line of march, and at the appointed hour the bugle call to

"Fall In"

Was sounded, and so perfect were the arrangements that within twenty minutes the grand cavalcade was on the march. Moving down Main street from Green the order of the column was as follows, as it passed the STANDARD Printing House: Grand Marshal I. G. Messee and Aids; Wm. Irwin's Artillery; Mexican Association; A. O. U. W. of Bodie; Veterans of the Late War; President, Orator, Poet and other officers of the day; Bodie Fire Department, the Babcock Engine leading, with the enticing Annie Medgerly, spendidly dressed, as Queen—An elegant turnout, and creditable to the largest metropolitan cities. Then followed the Pioneer Hook and Ladder company in fine condition, nicely decorated, with Master James Edward Tobin as King, and Miss Hettie Murphy as Queen—twenty members. Then came Champion Hose Company No. 1—thirty-six members. Their canopy was beautiful, and only excelled by the little Queen Gertie Smith. The Neptune Hose Company, No. 2, under the direction of Major Pat. Holland, was conspicuous and much admired, as was also the little Queen, Pearl Phillips, dressed in blue, scarlet and gold. This company numbered forty-five. Following them came the Booker Artillery, numbering ten men, weight on an average about forty pounds apiece, with Master Irwin, mounted, as Captain. The cannon, manufactured by order of Colonel Ellsworth was a splendid piece of workmanship, was mounted upon wheels, but its diminutiveness suggested to us the dividends occuring from the Comstock mines.

But the little fellows got along with it, and seemed to act as if their hold upon the Booker proposition was a good one. Following the Booker Artillery came

The Car of State,

Guarded, upon either side, by fourteen men of the Miners' Union, and, directly after it, two hundred more of the members of that organization, commanded by its President, Mr. Shaughnessy. Next followed the California and Bodie Base Ball Companies, citizens in carriages, the Bodie Butchers' Association, in a large carriage drawn by six finely caparisoned horses, with the brass band of Hoskins & Co., the Bulls-head, Bodie, City, Miners, and Union meat market wagons, splendidly decorated; the Pioneer Bakery, the Pioneer Brewery wagon, with the motto "They All Like It," Weber's blacksmith shop wagon, upon the sides of which was painted "We Do the Best Work in Mono County;" another wagon of Weber's carrying a live horse, upon which was being fastened, the shoes actually being forged upon the wagon; the Bodie Brewery wagon, with beer on tap; citizens in carriages—twelve of them; citizens mounted; and, as file-closers, came the Piutes, mounted, forty in number—that is, the horses, an Indian upon each, and in several instances two. The Indians seemed to have anticipated the situation and their horses were made variegated by means of paint.

Thousands of People.

Lined the streets, greater anthusiasm never before prevailed, singing and cheering from the balconies and re-echoed from the column being continuous from the commencement to the ending of the march. Counter-marching was necessary to bring all before the grand stand, each association cheering each other as they passed; but that which gave the most satisfaction to all present was the order of Mr. Shaughnessy, President of the Miners' Union, when he said: "Miners' Union, attention! Three cheers for Captain Messec, the Grand Marshal, and the officers of the day!" The cheers were given with a will by the gallant two hundred and fourteen who honored themselves and the National Day by turning out and making the fine display they did. The procession then broke ranks and soon appeared before

The Grand Stand,

Erected in front of the Gold Brick Saloon, on Main street, and, after having been called to order by the President of the day, Judge Marcus P. Wiggin.

The Following Prayer

Was offered to the Most High by Rev. G. B. Hinkle:

Almighty and Everlasting God our Heavenly Father, Heaven is Thy throne and earth is Thy footstool. Before Thy Majesty and Holiness the Angels veil their faces and the spirits of the just made perfect bow in humble adoration. Thou art the Creator of all things and the preserver of all that exists, whether they be thrones, or dominions or principalities. The minute and the vast, the atoms and worlds, all alike, attest the ubiquity of Thy presence and the Omnipotence of Thy power. Thou alone art the Sovereign Ruler of nations. The past, with all its records, is the unfolding of Thy counsels and the realization of Thy supreme designs. We adore Thee as our Supreme Ruler, the King Eternal, Immortal and Invincible; the only true God, blessed forevermore. We come on this great day, Oh Thou God of our Fathers, into Thy presence with praise and thanksgiving. We bless Thee for this day, for a national birth, and that we are permitted to convene to celebrate the one hundred and fourth anniversary of the same under such favorable circumstances. We praise Thee for the land which Thou gavest to our fathers—a land veiled for ages from the ancient world—but revealed in the fullness of time to our fathers a land of vast extent, of boundless resources, of great fertility and inexhaustible treasures. We thank Thee for the fathers of the country—men of might and mind—who endured hardships and privations to lay on the broad foundation of Truth and Justice, the grand structure of civil and religious freedom. We praise Thee for the founders of the government, for the immortal Washington and his noble and worthy associates and the service they rendered us and our posterity in handing down to us this great inheritance. Oh that we and posterity may prove ourselves worthy of the service rendered and the great gift bestowed. Again we would praise Thee for the material prosperity and development with which we have been blessed, the progress we have made in science, art and education, and for the degree of moral character we have been enabled by Thee to maintain. We praise Thee, Oh God, that though we have had war from without and within, and have been compelled to experience the sad effects of foreign and domestic strife, yet our government and nationality has been preserved. Oh God, wilt thou grant that it may be preserved through all coming time to bless the future generations that shall people the earth. Wilt Thou, Oh God, save us from the destroyer in the future, and may we be more strongly united in one great brotherhood in the time to come than in the past. May we ever remember that united we stand, divided we fall. We pray for Thy blessing, Oh God, to rest upon the President of these United States; may he have wisdom from above to guide him, and righteousness to adorn him, and firmness to maintain the right in vindication of truth and justice. Wilt Thou, Oh God, grant to every member of his Cabinet the grace of wisdom, temperance, honesty, truth and righteousness. We implore Thy blessing to rest upon the Legislative Department of our Nation. May just and righteous laws be enacted by them from time to time. We would commend to Thee our Judiciary. We pray that wisdom, firmness and justice may characterize their efforts in the administration of law, to the punishment of the guilty and the protection of the innocent. And we pray Thee, Oh God, to grant that when the responsibilities now resting on those who fill official positions in Church and State, shall be transferred to others, that they may be worthy of the positions to which they may be called. We also ask Thee to grant that they may have wisdom to guide them and Thy grace to influence thier hearts to do Thy will. And now we pray that when this day's celebration in commemoration of the event shall close, that we as American citizens may be more thoroughly imbued with christian purity and more strongly attached to, and appreciate more perfectly, our free institutions. Grant that we may know no East, no West, no North, no South, but our whole country, and be more strongly united than ever before in the bonds of brotherly love. All this we ask through the name of Him which was and which is and is to come, the only wise God, blessed forevermore; Amen.

After which the Bodie Brass Band discoursed a national air, and Mr. Alexander Hunter in as clear voice and forcible style as we have ever heard, read the Declaration of Independence. More music followed by the band, and the President of the Day introduced General John R. Kittrell, the Orator of the Day, who, in his masterly manner delivered the following

Oration.

[The principal portion of General Kittrell's oration will appear in to-morrow's issue of the STANDARD.—ED.]

After another national air by the band Mr. Alfred Graham recited an original poem which will be pulished hereafter. It was loudly applauded, and is creditable in every respect.

Rev. Mr. Hinkle dismissed the grand concourse of people with a blessing, and all departed for their homes, feeling satisfied that they had passed as good a Fourth of July in Bodie as is vouchsafed to people of large cities. All went home well pleased with the celebration, satisfied their hunger, and then returned to witness the march and exercises of

"The Horribles"

Who wound up the proceedings of the day, and it was horrible enough without any attempt upon our part to delineate the characters. Those who have seen them once know very well that there is but one role in which they can play. The out-turn pleased the boys and girls, and a few grown people were seen to "smile" audibly, while they were traversing Main street, up and down.

The Fire Works.

The Committee of Arrangements had purchased fire works to the amount of about $600. The works of itself, was good enough, but the distance they were placed from the town and the manner in which they were "touched off" lent but little interest to the celebration. Fireworks, unless on a very extensive scale, and properly managed, will use up money on a Fourth of July faster than anything we know of, and as a general thing, an investment of only a few hundred dollars is money thrown away.

Incidents.

Nearly all the hoisting works buildings, the boarding-houses and many private dwellings on Bodie Hill were gaily bedecked with the American colors. One large flag attracted particular attention. It was flying from a staff set on the highest point of Bodie Bluff. The Committee of Arrangements had determined that the flag should be there, but, as they had neither staff or flag, for the moment they were nonplussed. They were not to be outdone, however, for they put their wits to work, and picking up a piece of staff here and another there they had them spliced together and soon a very good staff was supplied. The material for the flag was picked up in a similar manner, and a full-sized garrison flag was flying from the staff. The work of manufacturing the staff and flag and planting on the Bluff was commenced at noon of Sunday, and by 4 o'clock P. M. the flag was flying. The Committee are entitled to great credit for their thoughtfulness in placing a flag there as also for the expeditious manner in which the work was done. J. T. Clark made the staff, and it is a nice piece of work. The little

Representatives of the States and Territories

Desire to return their kindest thanks to C. A. Richardson and Joseph Falkingham, who were thoughtful and considerate enough to have prepared a large quantity of lemonade, with which the little ones' thirst was quenched. Such acts of kindness are never forgotten by children. Many other incidents, of an interesting nature occurred during the day, but we have not space in to-day's issue to give them notice.

Accident.

The only accident we could learn of happened to George Hanscom, who was cabining with some of the employes of the STANDARD office on the hillside south of Lowe street. He got up early in the morning, and, by the aid of an old anvil, was going to give the boys a salute. He inserted a heavy charge of powder and tamped a piece of fuse into the anvil and then set fire to the fuse. The thing did not seem to work as fast as Hanscom thought it ought to, and he went back to see what was the matter with it. When standing immediately over it the explosion occurred, bursting the anvil and throwing the pieces in every direction, and filling the face and eyes of Hanscom with powder. Dr. Roger and Son were immediately called, and while they find that Hanscom is severely burned, yet they think his eyesight is not destroyed. Except for this accident, nothing occurred to mar the harmony of the grandest celebration ever had in a mining camp.

The following additional news item about an impromptu Independence Day celebration appeared in the *Daily Bodie Standard* on Thursday, July 15, 1880.

GENERAL NOTES.

A man named Rogers, while sitting in a saloon at Moore's Flat, Nevada county, last Sunday, celebrated the Fourth by laying his revolver across his knee and without taking aim, firing five shots at a crowd of men in a store across the street. He said it was done for the fun of the thing.

News item from Moore's Flat, California.

III:
"Good-by, God…"

While the famous riposte to the smear on Bodie's reputation is widely known (page 24), the lesser-known first rebuttal by a local paper was both indignant and equally clever.

DAILY BODIE STANDARD

VOL. I.   BODIE, MONO COUNTY, CALIFORNIA. THURSDAY. FEBRUARY 13, 1879.   NO. 71.

"Good-by, God; we are going to Bodie in the morning," was the suggestive termination of a sweet little three-year old's prayer the other evening at San Jose, just prior to the departure of the family for the wicked mining camp mentioned. Not bad, that, but rather severe on Bodie.—*Nevada Tribune*. All right, pardner; but we have no particular use here for a god that confines himself to the limits of San Jose; and we don't wonder that even a little three-year-old was willing to say "good-bye" when she thought she had a chance to get out of that delectable place in order to come to Bodie

An indignant and equally clever reply to the smear on Bodie's reputation.

The *Daily Bodie Standard* did not let things go with the response shown on page 95. It returned the favor with the following editorial remark in the same February 13, 1879 issue. The "deals" mentioned could well have included the infamous stock fraud that helped bring down Aurora's boom in 1864.

> Nevada mining "deals" have caused more men to go crazy than those of any other State in the Union, and yet she will not provide for a State Insane Asylum. It is not an agricultural State, and that, probably, is the reason she wants to "farm" things out.

Returning Nevada Tribune's editorial favor.

IV:
REMINISCENCES OF BUCKSKIN JOE

As noted in "A Lady Called Silver Heels" in Chapter Two, the Park County seat moved from Buckskin Joe to Fairplay, approximately seven miles away, when the former town was in decline. The account below was published about ten years after Buckskin Joe's abandonment and mentioned neither a smallpox outbreak nor the legend of Silver Heels.

One excerpt on the following page relates how Lauret was named; the other contains the only reference to "Silver Heels" found in the author's search of the period from the camp's founding through its `heyday.

THE FAIRPLAY FLUME.

VOL. 1.   FAIRPLAY, PARK COUNTY, COLORADO, THURSDAY, JUNE 19, 1879.   NO. 18.

Reminiscences of Buckskin Joe.

Passing the site of the old town of Buckskin, (or, as it was formerly called, of Buckskin Joe,) in company with Judge N. J. Bond, who was one of the pioneers of that district, he pointed out to a representative of the FLUME many interesting points in that notable locality and recalled so many reminiscences of the days and years when Buckskin Joe was "booming" that had note book and pencil been at hand we could have furnished an interesting and lengthy article. Unfortunately only a part can be remembered. It was in '61 that the remarkable mineral discoveries in Buckskin gulch drew an immense number of miners to that locality, and a busy bustling mining town of two thousand population soon sprang up. While the excitement was at its height the placer mining excitement of California gulch was just beginning to wane and the miners and prospectors kept coming in from there at rate of seventy-five to a hundred and twenty-five a day. The Judge pointed out the remains of a chimney, all that was left of the building in which the mining laws of the district were drawn up. Under these laws, which were as faithfully observed as if they had been lawfully inscribed on the statute books, the locator of a claim was allowed but one hundred feet of territory along the vein. Guided by such landmarks as a few rotten timbers or stones used for foundations, he pointed out the site of the theater building, the grand hotel and several smaller public houses, billiard halls, stores, saloons, stage office, postoffice and the bank of Stansell, Bond & Harris, in fact we were traversing the main street of the town, silent and deserted now but then humming with excitement. Then Tabor was an unpretentious grocer; satisfied to turn a penny by any means. He occupied a small store, carried a small stock and was considered a not overly great man, and J. B. Stansell, who was last summer door tender at one of the Leadville theaters, was then a bonanza king of Buckskin Joe. One small cabin alone remains on the street. One would hesitate to give five dollars for it now, but then it found ready sale at a thousand. Of nine stamp mills whose seventy-two stamps created ceaseless din and in two years ground out shining gold to the value of half a million dollars, only one tumble-down structure is left. In the whole town there are not to exceed ten buildings left. These are the changes that years bring about. Yet, strange to say, the mines are rich as ever, and though idle so long they are likely to remain so no longer.

An account of an 1879 visit to the ghost town of Buckskin Joe, Colorado.
The one-column article was digitally arranged to fit the pages of this book.

DAILY ROCKY MOUNTAIN NEWS.

VOLUME 1.   DENVER, TUESDAY EVENING, SEPTEMBER 18, 1860.   NUMBER 20.

For the Rocky Mountain News.
From the Silver Mines.

LAURET, BUCKSKIN JOE GULCH, }
September, 9th, '60. }

EDS. NEWS:—From the above date you will perceive I hail from a gulch deriving its name from a mountaineer of some note, who has made several discoveries of quartz and mineral leads hereabouts. The town (Lauret) was so named by a meeting of the citizens a few days since at the Recorder's office. The desire was to have named it by compounding the names of the only two ladies in the gulch,(for there are two here, God bless them,) wives of the two Dodge Brothers. One however objecting, the above was adopted as a compromise for Lauranette.

This gulch is upon a branch of the South Platte and about five miles long, with a pleasant valley from a quarter to half a mile wide, with mostly good grazing land. The gulch diggings are not remunerative, being very stony and hard to work. Some days men do tolerably well, but not generally.

The number of leads already discovered and on record in this short gulch is twenty-one. In some ten of them there is found a combination of white metal claimed to be silver—but of this we hope to be better satisfied in a few days. The quartz is said to be rich. I have not yet seen any prospecting results, and can only speak from reports, which are not always reliable. I am pleased to say, however, that I find, as a general thing, some of the most worthy men here that I have met anywhere in the mountains. Should these mines prove as valuable as supposed to be, there will hardly be an equal to it anywhere in the mountains. It is easy of access—sixty miles from Colorado, twenty from Tarryall, sixteen from Breckenridge, and fifteen from California Gulch. The north branch of the Platte affords additional pasturage for stock.

ROCKY MOUNTAIN NEWS.

THE MINES AND MINERS OF KANSAS AND NEBRASKA.

VOL. 1.   AURARIA AND DENVER, K. T., THURSDAY, OCTOBER 20, 1859.   NO. 22.

For the Rocky Mountain News.
ST. LOUIS, Oct. 3, 1859.

Editor News.

SIR:—Our party reached this city on Sunday, 25th September, just in time to be at the commencement of the Eclipse Fair. Some of the prizes, you are aware, amounted to $1,000 each. The largest, I believe, ever offered by any association. The Fair has been largely attended, and the receipts at the gate reached the sum of $31,000, besides the amount paid for rent of Booths, which was upwards of $9,000. There were no entrance fees for articles or stock.—Everything was free as air for exhibitors. The awards very generally gave satisfaction. The number of entries of live stock were upwards of seven hundred. The show of cattle which has heretofore not been very extensive, was the finest that ever collected at any place in this country.

The great prize of $1,000, for best bull, was taken by R. A. Alexander, of Woodford county, Kentucky. Another prize of same value as this was awarded to Cooper & Crane, of Ohio, for best roadster stallion. This celebrated trotting steed is of wonderful fine form, and possesses all the points necessary to a perfect roadster. There were upwards of forty entries for this premium, among which I noticed the swift footed "Silver Heels," "Flying Cloud," "Henry Clay," "Green Mountain," "Black Hawk," "Hamiltonian," "Ed. Forrest," "Peerless," "Addison," "White Mountain," and many others worthy of note. There was a severe test in examining the points of the different competitors, which was narrowed down after two hours hard driving to "Green Mountain," of Ky., and "Stockbridge Chief," of Ohio. The palm of victory was awarded at last to the Ohio horse.

Naming of Lauret (top) and an obscure reference to the name "Silver Heels" (bottom). Both articles are excerpts and were digitally arranged to fit the pages of this book.

BIBLIOGRAPHY

"Local Intelligence: Another Growl." *Bodie Chronicle,* 17 July 1880, p. 3.
Bodie State Historic Park. California State Parks, 1988.
Bright, William. *1500 California Place Names: Their Origin and Meaning* (A revised version of *1000 California Place Names* by Erwin G. Gudde, third edition). Berkeley, CA: University of California Press, 1998.
Brown, Dee. *Bury My Heart at Wounded Knee: An Indian History of the American West.* New York, NY: Holt, Rinehart & Winston, Inc., 1970.
Brown, Robert L. *Ghost Towns of the Colorado Rockies.* Caldwell, ID: Caxton Printers, 1969.
---. *Jeep Trails to Colorado Ghost Towns.* Caldwell, ID: Caxton Printers, 1963.
Bodie State Historic Park. California State Parks, 2018.
Marshall Gold Discovery State Historic Park. California State Parks, 2013.
Capps, Benjamin. *The Old West: The Great Chiefs.* New York, NY: Time-Life Books, 1975.
Cerney, Jan, and Robert Sago in cooperation with the Minnilusa Historical Association. *Black Hills Gold Rush Towns.* Charleston, SC: Arcadia Publishing, 2010.
"Bodie in New York." *Daily Bodie Standard,* 26 Mar. 1880, p. 3.
"Brief Mention." *Daily Bodie Standard,* 15 July 1880, p. 3.
"The Celebration in Bodie." *Daily Bodie Standard,* 6 July 1880, p. 3.
"General Notes." *Daily Bodie Standard,* 15 July 1880, p. 2.
"Slanderous." *Daily Bodie Standard,* 13 Feb. 1879, p. 3.
"From the Silver Mines." *Daily Rocky Mountain News,* 18 Sept. 1860, p. 2.
"Cyanide Heap Leach Packet." *Earthworks,* August 2000, www.earthworks.org/cms/assets/uploads/archive/files/publications/Cyanide_Leach_Packet.pdf.
Ely, Sims. *The Lost Dutchman Mine: The Fabulous Story of the Seven-Decade Search for the Hidden Treasure in the Superstition Mountains of Arizona.* New York, NY: William Morrow and Company, 1953.
"Reminiscences of Buckskin Joe." *The Fairplay Flume,* 19 June 1879, p. 2.

Feldman, Ron. *Crooked Mountain.* Apache Junction, AZ: World Publishing Corp., 2000.

Fifer, Barbara. *Montana Mining Ghost Towns.* Helena, MT: Farcountry Press, 2002.

Finley, Bruce. "One of Colorado's worst Superfund sites has been fixed, but the State's on the hook for $2M a year to keep it clean." *The Denver Post,* 10 July 2018, www.denverpost.com/2018/07/10/colorado-summitville-mine-cleanup/. Accessed 3 Dec. 2018.

Florin, Lambert. *Ghost Towns of the West.* New York, NY: Promontory Press, 1993.

Geissinger, Terri Lynn. *Bodie: 1859-1962.* Charleston, SC: Arcadia Publishing, 2009.

Glover, T. E. *The Lost Dutchman Mine of Jacob Waltz.* Phoenix, AZ: Cowboy-Miner Productions, 1998.

---. *The Lost Dutchman Mine of Jacob Waltz-Part 2: The Holmes Manuscript.* Phoenix, AZ: Cowboy-Miner Productions, 2000.

Hafen, LeRoy R., editor. *Colorado Gold Rush: Contemporary Letters and Reports 1858-1859.* Glendale, CA: The Arthur H. Clark Company, 1941.

Hogan, Elizabeth L., editor. *Gold Rush Country.* Menlo Park, CA: Lane Publishing Co., 1972 (4th edition, updated 1989).

"The Discovery of Gold in California." *Hutchings' California Magazine.* Nov. 1857: pp. 200-201.

Jessen, Kenneth. *Ghost Towns, Colorado Style: Volume Two-Central Region.* Loveland, CO: J. V. Publications, 1999.

---. *Ghost Towns, Colorado Style: Volume Three-Southern Region.* Loveland, CO: J. V. Publications, 2001.

Johnson, Russ and Anne Johnson. *The Ghost Town of Bodie.* Bishop, CA: Community Printing and Publishing, 1998.

Ketellapper, Victor. "First Five Year Review Report for Summitville Mine Superfund Site." *United States Environmental Protection Agency,* 3 Aug. 2000, semspub.epa.gov/work/08/490202.pdf.

King, Clarence. *Mountaineering in the Sierra Nevada.* New York, NY: Charles Scribner's Sons, 1871 (revised 1902).

Knight, Arthur Winfield. "The Great Republic of Rough and Ready." *Anderson Valley Advertiser,* 10 Oct. 2003, www.theava.com/03/0910-roughready.html.

Ghosts of the West: Stampede on the Bonanza Trail. Directed by E. S. Knightchilde. Knight Sky Pictures, in production.

Ghosts of the West: The End of the Bonanza Trail. Directed by E. S. Knightchilde. Knight Sky Pictures, 2012.

Mather, R. E. and R. E. Boswell. "Henry Plummer." *Historynet,* www.historynet.com/henry-plummer.htm. Accessed 28 Nov. 2018.

"Ghost Town." *Merriam-Webster.* www.merriam-webster.com/dictionary/ghost%20town. Accessed 8 Dec. 2018.

Miller, Donald C. *Ghost Towns of Montana: A Classic Tour Through the Treasure State's Historical Sites.* Guilford, CT: TwoDot, 2008.

Mitchell, John D. *Lost Mines of the Great Southwest.* Glorietta, NM: The Rio Grande Press, 1933.

Bannack. Montana Fish, Wildlife & Parks, 2009.

Mumey, Nolie. *History and Legal Proceedings of Buckskin Joe, C.T. 1859-1862.* Boulder, CO: The Johnson Publishing Co., 1961.

Murbarger, Nell. *Ghosts of the Glory Trail.* Los Angeles, CA: Westernlore Press, 1956.

Nadeau, Remi. *Ghost Towns and Mining Camps of California: A History & Guide.* Santa Barbara, CA: Crest Publishers, 1965 (revised 1992).

Nevin, David. *The Old West: The Expressmen.* New York, NY: Time-Life Books, 1974.

"Cyanide-Spill Suit is Settled in Colorado." *The New York Times*, March 2, 2001, www.nytimes.com/2000/12/24/us/cyanide-spill-suit-is-settled-in-colorado.html.

O'Neal, Bill. *Ghost Towns of the American West.* Lincolnwood, IL: Publications International, Lt., 1995.

Paher, Stanley W. *Nevada Ghost Towns and Mining Camps.* Las Vegas, NV: Nevada Publications, 1970.

Patterson, Amy. "Guide to Bodie Consolidated Mining Company Records." *California State Parks,* 2003, www.parks.ca.gov/pages/1080/files/fa_324_001.pdf.

Piatt, Michael H. "Correcting Recent Bodie Myths: Let's Set the Historic Record Straight." *History of Bodie, California: Mining Ghost Town Comes Alive.* www.bodiehistory.com/myths.pdf. Accessed 12 Feb. 2018.

---. "What the Historic Record Reveals about Bodie's Peak Population." *History of Bodie, California: Mining Ghost Town Comes Alive.* www.bodiehistory.com/Population.pdf. Accessed 12 Feb. 2018.

Plumlee, Geoffrey S. "Open File Report 95-0023: The Summitville Mine and Its Downstream Effects," *U.S. Geological Survey,* 11 July 1995, pubs.usgs.gov/of/1995/ofr-95-0023/summit.htm.

"Editor News." *Rocky Mountain News,* 20 Oct. 1859, p. 2.

Roosevelt, Theodore. *An Autobiography.* New York, NY: The Macmillan Company, 1913.

Shaw, Clifford Alpheus. *Aurora, Nevada: 1860-1960.* North Charleston, SC: CreateSpace Independent Publishing Platform, 2018 (2nd edition).

---. Personal Correspondence. 3 Oct. 2018 through 15 Mar. 2019.

Silver, Sue. *Aurora: Nevada's Silent City on the Hill.* North Charleston, SC: CreateSpace Independent Publishing Platform, 2018.

---. Personal Correspondence. 12 June 2015 through 20 Aug. 2018.

Smith, Carter, editor. *Riches of the West: A Sourcebook on the American West.* Brookfield, CT: The Millbrook Press, 1992.

Till, Tom and Teresa Jordan. *Great Ghost Towns of the West*. Portland, OR: Graphic Arts Center Publishing, 2001.

Twain, Mark. *Roughing It*. Hartford, CT: American Publishing Company, 1872.

"Report on Population of the United States at the Eleventh Census." *United States Census Bureau*, www.census.gov/prod/www/decennial.html.

"The Seventh Census of the United States: 1850." *United States Census Bureau*, www.census.gov/library/publications/1853/dec/1850a.html.

"Statistics of the Population of the United States at the Tenth Census." *United States Census Bureau*, www.census.gov/prod/www/decennial.html.

"Thirteenth Census of the United States Taken in the Year 1910." *United States Census Bureau*, www.census.gov/prod/www/decennial.html.

"Twelfth Census of the United States Taken in the Year 1900." *United States Census Bureau*, www.census.gov/prod/www/decennial.html.

Varney, Phillip. *Ghost Towns of California*. Minneapolis, MN: The Voyageur Press, 2012.

Wallace, Robert. *The Old West: The Miners*. Alexandria, Virginia: Time-Life Books, 1976.

Wheeler, Keith. *The Old West: The Chroniclers*. New York, NY: Time-Life Books, 1976.

Williams, Mark. *Landscapes and Water (GEOG 1011): Summitville Mine Disaster*. University of Colorado Boulder. snobear.colorado.edu/Markw/Intro/Summitville/summitville.html.

Willison, George F. *Here They Dug the Gold*. New York, NY: A. L. Burt Company, 1931.

Wolle, Muriel Sibell. *The Bonanza Trail: Ghost Towns and Mining Camps of the West*. Bloomington, IN: Indiana University Press, 1953.

---. *Montana Pay Dirt: A Guide to the Mining Camps of the Treasure State*. Athens, OH: Swallow Press/Ohio University Press, 1963.

---. *Stampede to Timberline: The Ghost Towns and Mining Camps of Colorado*. Denver, CO: Sage Books, 1949.

---. *Timberline Tailings: Tales of Colorado's Ghost Towns and Mining Camps*. Chicago, IL: Swallow Press, 1977.

Wright, Christie. *All That Lies Beneath*. 2nd ed., San Francisco, CA: Blurb, 2012.

---. Personal Correspondence. 7 July 2015 through 10 Mar. 2019.

Young, John P. *San Francisco: A History of the Pacific Coast Metropolis, Vol. I*. Chicago: The S. J. Clarke Publishing Co., 1912.

PHOTO CREDITS

Attributions for archival images are listed below. All current photographs appearing in this volume and on the covers were taken by the author and Todd Prescott.

Page 7: Courtesy of California State University, Chico, Meriam Library Special Collections.
Page 10: Courtesy of U.S. National Archives and Records Administration.
Page 11: Courtesy of U.S. National Archives and Records Administration.
Page 12: Courtesy of U.S. National Archives and Records Administration.
Page 13: Combined from two photos that were separately published in *San Francisco: A History of the Pacific Coast Metropolis, Vol. 1* and retrieved from archive.org/details/sanfranciscohist01youn/page/n217.
Page 18 (top): Public domain image retrieved from Wikimedia Commons and digitally enhanced for publication. Original retrieved from commons.wikimedia.org/wiki/File:HenryPlummer.jpg.
Page 18 (bottom): Courtesy of The New York Public Library Digital Collections.
Page 20: Public domain image retrieved from Wikimedia Commons and digitally enhanced for publication. Original retrieved from commons.wikimedia.org/wiki/File:Charles_P_Chuck_Stanton_Arizona.jpg.
Page 23: Courtesy of University of Nevada, Reno, Nevada in Maps collection, digitally edited for publication.
Page 24: Courtesy of the California History Room, California State Library, Sacramento, California.
Page 25: Courtesy of U.S. National Archives and Records Administration, digitally edited for publication.
Page 26: Extracted from microfilm records provided courtesy of California State Library, Sacramento, California.
Page 27: Courtesy of Mono County Historical Society.
Page 28: Courtesy of Mono County Historical Society.
Page 29: Courtesy of Park County Local History Archives.

Page 30: Courtesy of Park County Local History Archives.
Page 31 (top): Courtesy of Park County Local History Archives.
Page 34: Courtesy of Park County Local History Archives.
Page 38: Courtesy of Granite County Museum & Cultural Center.
Page 39: Courtesy of Montana Historical Society Research Center.
Page 40 (top left): Courtesy of Library of Congress Prints and Photographs Division.
Page 42: Courtesy of Denver Public Library, Western History Collection.
Page 43: Courtesy of Denver Public Library, Western History Collection.
Page 45: Courtesy of Central Nevada Historical Society.
Page 46 (top): Courtesy of Nevada Historical Society.
Page 46 (bottom): Courtesy of University of Nevada, Reno Special Collections and University Archives.
Page 47: Courtesy of Nevada Historical Society.
Page 48 (top): Courtesy of University of Nevada, Reno Special Collections and University Archives.
Page 48 (bottom): Courtesy of Mono County Historical Society.
Page 49: Courtesy of Central Nevada Historical Society.
Page 52 (top): Courtesy of Nevada Historical Society.
Page 53 (top): Courtesy of Nevada Historical Society.
Page 54 (top): Courtesy of Mono County Historical Society.
Page 55 (top): Courtesy of the California History Room, California State Library, Sacramento, California.
Page 55 (middle): Courtesy of California Geological Survey.
Page 56: Courtesy of Library of Congress Prints and Photographs Division.
Page 67: Courtesy of University of Nevada, Reno Special Collections and University Archives.
Page 68 (top): Courtesy of Nevada Historical Society.
Page 68 (bottom): Courtesy of Central Nevada Historical Society.
Page 69 (top): Courtesy of University of Nevada, Reno Special Collections and University Archives.
Page 69 (bottom): Courtesy of Central Nevada Historical Society.
Page 70 (top): Courtesy of Central Nevada Historical Society.
Page 70 (bottom): Courtesy of Library of Congress Prints and Photographs Division.
Pages 89-96: Extracted from microfilm records provided courtesy of California State Library, Sacramento, California.
Pages 97-98: Extracted from digitized records provided courtesy of www.ColoradoHistoricNewspapers.org.

MORE ON THE GHOST TOWNS OF THE OLD WEST

Interested in seeing more from the Ghosts of the West project? To inquire about a lecture or screening for your group or to peruse the online store, visit KnightSkyPictures.com, or write to Knight Sky Pictures, 215 W. Riverside Dr #992, Estes Park, CO 80517. A selection of products, with prices as of June 2023, appears on the following pages.

Ghosts of the West: The End of the Bonanza Trail **DVD**

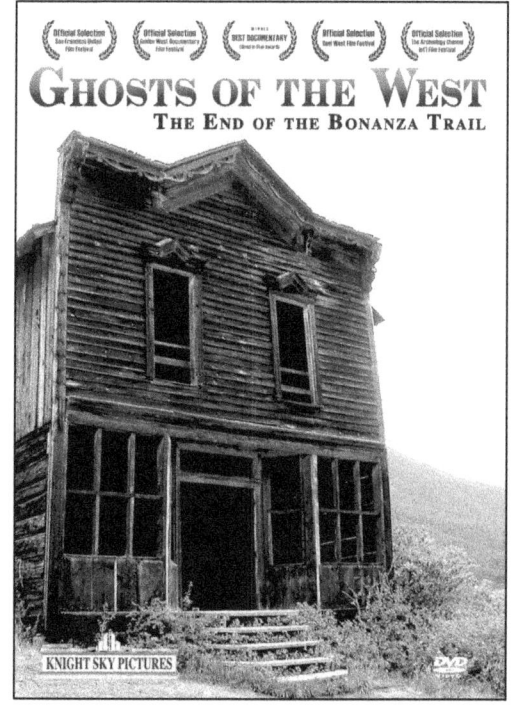

The Best Documentary Award-winning feature, presented uncut in its original theatrical aspect ratio.

Extras include approximately fifteen minutes of deleted scenes and interviews, including Disaster at Summitville, The Decline of Silver Cliff, The Lost Blue Bucket Mine, and more!

The fifty-seven-minute feature is available as a stand-alone DVD or as a DVD & CD soundtrack combo. Starting at $20.

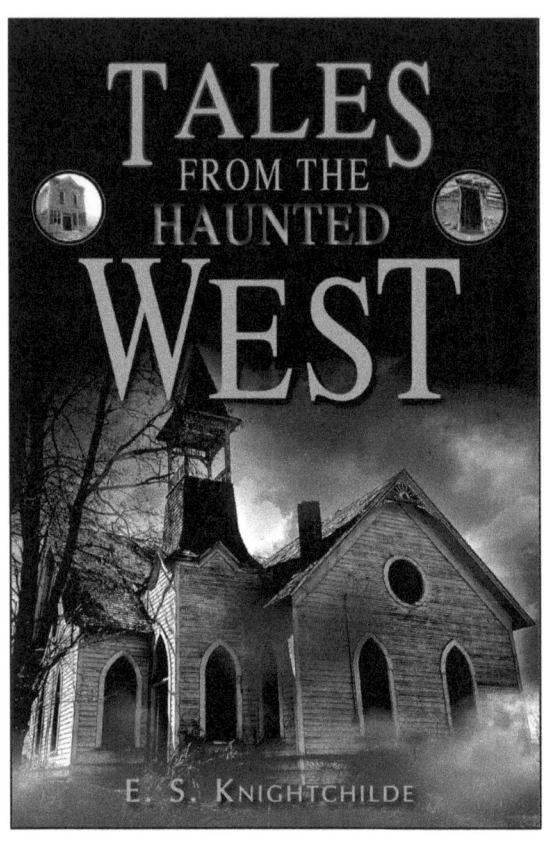

Tales from the Haunted West

Anecdotes, stories, and photographs drawn from more than twenty years of travel to hundreds of ghost towns throughout the West.

Accompanied by dozens of images, this short book presents a collection of tales from the somber to the supernatural, of history both real and imagined, of ghost towns, and of ghosts that yet may linger.

The trade paperback measures 6 by 9 inches, has full-color covers, and contains 50 black & white pages. $11.

The Ghost Town Tee Shirt, Colorado edition

The limited-run Ghost Town Tee Shirt features the poster art for *Ghosts of the West: The End of the Bonanza Trail* with "Colorado" in large letters above and behind a spectacular, abandoned 1880s hotel.

The dark heather tee is available in four sizes (S, M, L, XL) while supplies last. $22

Ghosts of the West Original Motion Picture Soundtrack Album CD

Looking for the perfect music to accompany your ghost town and Old West reading and exploring?

Adrian L. Hernandez's acclaimed score for *Ghosts of the West* captures the extremes of the Old West beautifully, along with the sense of nostalgia that we, generations removed, have for the era. The CD contains the entirety of the film's score, presented in its proper order, and comes in a full-color, eco-friendly, space-saving cardboard sleeve. All musicians involved would go on to perform at the 2013 Presidential Inauguration.

$11 (or at a discount as part of a movie combo).

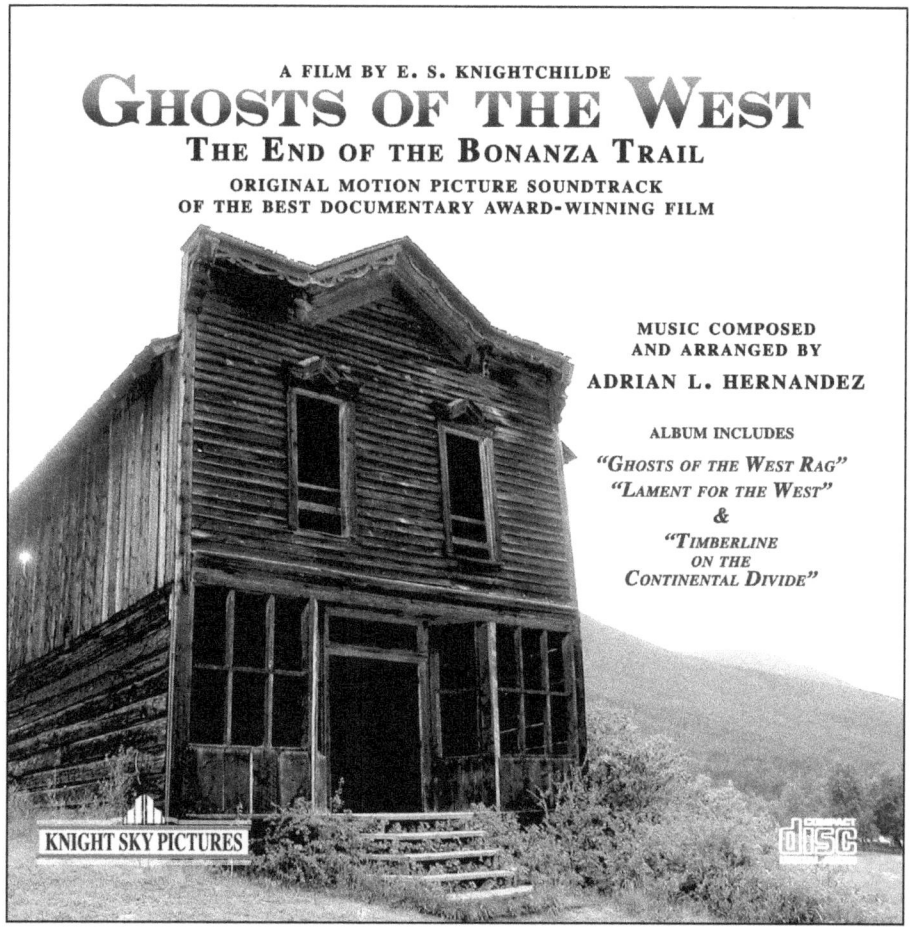

Vintage Style *"Greetings from"* Postcards

Send a postcard through time!

These cards feature a vintage look with a full-color front side. On the "Greetings from the Old West, USA" card, each letter contains an iconic image of a ghost town, mining camp, or landscape from across the western states. "Greetings from Bodie, CAL." includes photos of famous facades and interiors from the world-renowned site.

Printed on sturdy 14 pt. stock to survive mailing, the postcards measure 4.25" x 6" and feature a high gloss front that makes the art stand out with an uncoated back for ease of writing a greeting and address. Available in packages of 10 for $10.

Ghosts of the West **Production Stills** – Peruse a set of haunting images from location shooting for the first installment of *Ghosts of the West*. Color and sepia, matted and metal, signed and numbered, limited edition prints start at $29.

ABOUT THE AUTHOR

E. S. Knightchilde is the writer-director of Best Documentary Award-winner, *Ghosts of the West: The End of the Bonanza Trail,* and the multi-award-winning short, *Not for Today, But for All Time*…. He has presented multimedia lectures about ghost towns to capacity crowds and is currently working on the next installment in the *Ghosts of the West* film series, subtitled *Stampede on the Bonanza Trail.*

Knightchilde has traveled tens of thousands of miles over the last two decades to film and photograph hundreds of ghost towns and mining camps of the Old West. He is a former President of the Ghost Town Club of Colorado (ghosttownclub.org) and resides in the Rocky Mountains.

E. S. Knightchilde filming for Ghosts of the West at South Park City Museum, Fairplay, Colorado. Courtesy of Karl Johnson.

www.ingramcontent.com/pod-product-compliance
Lightning Source LLC
Chambersburg PA
CBHW061209070526
44583CB00025B/3179